I0796851

SPIRIT MAGIC

© Jessamyn Harris

Phoenix LeFae (she/her) started her journey in the world of Witchcraft in 1993 when her athame was a wooden-handled butter knife stolen from her mom's kitchen. Her love of magick and mystery has led her down many paths, lineages, and traditions. She is an initiate in the Reclaiming Tradition of Witchcraft, the Avalon Druid Order, and Gardnerian Wicca. Phoenix has written several books, including *What Is Remembered Lives, A Witch's Guide to Creating and Performing Rituals, Witches, Heretics & Warrior Women,* and more. She is a professional Witch and the owner of the esoteric Goddess shop Milk & Honey, www.Milk-and-Honey.com. Find out more at www.phoenixlefae.com.

SPIRIT MAGIC

ELEMENTS OF WITCHCRAFT

PHOENIX LEFAE

WOODBURY, MINNESOTA

FIRST EDITION
First Printing, 2026

Cover design by Shannon McKuhen
Interior illustrations by Llewellyn Art Department
Tarot Original 1909 Deck © 2021 with art created by Pamela Colman Smith
and Arthur Edward Waite. Used with permission of LoScarabeo.

Library of Congress Cataloging-In-Publication Data (Pending)
ISBN: 978-0-7387-7940-9

Llewellyn Publications
A Division of Llewellyn Worldwide Ltd.
2143 Wooddale Drive
Woodbury, MN 55125-2989

www.llewellyn.com
Printed in the United States of America

GPSR Representation:
UPI-2M PLUS d.o.o., Medulićeva 20, 10000 Zagreb, Croatia
matt.parsons@upi2mbooks.hr

This book is dedicated to my partner
and biggest cheerleader,
Gwion Raven

CONTENTS

"Nature always wears the colors of the spirit."

—Ralph Waldo Emerson, Nature, *1836*

DISCLAIMER

This book is not intended as medical or psychological advice. Any activities suggested here should be approached with care and caution. If you require medical assistance or mental or physical care, please seek help from professionals. Avoid performing any rituals or practices in this book if they could cause you harm, either physical or psychological. Refrain from using any items suggested in this book if you are allergic or uncertain about a possible allergic reaction. Herbs that are marked as poisonous are provided solely for informational purposes. Do not use them.

FOREWORD: THE UNKNOWABLE FORCE OF SPIRIT

For centuries and through many esoteric practices, the elements have been the cornerstones of magical practice. Whether it's ancient astrology or modern Witchcraft, these four basic elements create the boundaries and structures for larger, multidimensional spiritual frameworks.

Earth is the ground we walk on, quite literally. It is the rocks, the mud, and the mountains. Earth is also our body and our physical manifestation in this life. Earth is our center, our money, and our stability.

Fire is the flame in the hearth. It is the candle, the bonfire, the sun. Fire both warms and destroys. It has the power to transform and incite. Fire is the flame of passion and our will to go on.

Water is the rain from the skies. It is the world's oceans, lakes, and rivers. It is a comforting bath and the morning dew. Water is our blood, sweat, and tears. It rules our emotions and manifests as memories.

Air is all around us. It is the sounds we hear and the wind that touches our faces. Air carries seeds and pollen and the scents that both warn and delight. Air is our voice, our thoughts, and our ideas.

But in many traditions and esoteric practices, there is also a fifth element: Spirit. It is the merger of all the elements, yet it is far more than the sum of those parts.

Spirit is unknowable yet all around us. It is untouchable, yet it is us. It is an essence, our soul, and that aetheric thing that gives everything life.

For modern Witches, Spirit can be found at the center of the magic circle and the celebratory Wheel of the Year. It spins in ritual as calls to deity are made and whispers to the soul in meditation and divination. In the occult world, Spirit is represented by the six-pointed star, which is a blend of the alchemical symbols for the four elements. For still others, Spirit can be found in a walk through the forest in the movement of plants, the call of animals, and the energy of the land.

This book is the fifth and final in a series that dives deep into the symbolism and spiritual use of the elements. The first four books, beginning with Water, highlighted each of the building blocks that make up Spirit. This one brings it all together, covering everything associated with the element of Spirit, from spiritual places and deities to practical spells and rituals.

Written by five different authors from around the globe, the Elements of Witchcraft series will show you just how wide and deep the esoteric understanding of the elements goes and how to make their fundamental lessons work for your own magical and spiritual needs.

Join us on a deep exploration and journey of the magical use of the four—no, five—elements.

By Heather Greene
Acquisitions Editor, Llewellyn Worldwide

INTRODUCTION: THE FIFTH ELEMENT

When I first started practicing Witchcraft, I was taught that Spirit exists in all the elements and all the elements exist in Spirit. Spirit is the all and the nothing, the deepest reaches of space. It is dark matter, which holds the universe together, meaning we don't totally understand it. Spirit is ineffable—it cannot truly be described because it is a thing that is beyond the use of words. Spirit is the center of the circle, the animating force that keeps us alive, and the stuff magic is made of. Spirit is the elusive fifth element.

When it comes to Spirit within the framework of modern Witchcraft, we have to ask if acknowledging this "fifth" element is necessary. In many Witchcraft traditions, Spirit isn't called or honored in a ritual framework. Where you might see invocations (or evocations) to the elements of Earth, Air, Fire, and Water, Spirit is often left out. And yet there are plenty of other traditions where there *is* a calling to Spirit, even if that is just with a silent nod or a pentacle drawn in the center of the ritual circle. In this inclusion and exclusion, we see a reminder that Spirit is a paradox.

In Western Witchcraft traditions, the other elements have directional assignments. Air is generally connected to the East, Fire to the South, Water to the West, and Earth to the North. So where is Spirit?

Spirit, of course, is in all these directions and all these elements; Spirit is the guardian of the center. Sounds simple enough, except for the fact that *center* is a moving target. The center isn't the same place for every person. My center is here within me and your center is there within you, and yet they are both center. There is a center of a ritual circle and at the same time there is a center of the ritual space—and these may or may not be the same place.

Spirit in an Esoteric Context

Many Western Witchcraft traditions also connect the elements to the directions and the directions to a guardian of a Watchtower that resides in that direction. Each element is called into ritual by calling upon the power of each of these Watchtowers.

The concept of the Watchtowers originated in the writings of John Dee and Edward Kelley, who worked magic in the 1500s involving angels, which is now referred to as Enochian magic. John Dee was the court astrologer for Elizabeth I, and Edward Kelley was a famous occultist. They explored the concept of an angel guarding and protecting each cardinal direction and the element associated with that direction. Earth is the realm of Uriel, Air is connected to Raphael, Fire is the realm of Michael, and Water is connected to Gabriel. The Hermetic Order of the Golden Dawn, formed in 1888, then popularized this idea.

But there isn't a Watchtower for Spirit because there isn't a Watchtower in the center, so does that mean it's not a traditional element?

Of course, this elusive nature is part of the thrill of working with Spirit as an elemental force. It is paradoxical and magically slippery.

Although one might argue that Wicca is an offshoot of Western Witchcraft, this system views the concept of Spirit as connected to matter. Wicca is an Earth religion that views the four elements as matter, and Spirit should not be separated from matter, meaning there is no reason to acknowledge Spirit as the fifth element because it is already inherently connected to the four material elements. Matter and Spirit are intertwined and impossible to pull apart.

Outside of the Witchcraft traditions inspired by Western occult practices, animism looks at everything in the world (the universe) as having its own inherent Spirit. Many modern traditions of Witchcraft are moving closer to an animistic worldview, honoring everything around us as alive and possessing Spirit. Is this view of Spirit the same as or different from a directional Spirit? And does it matter?

If we look to the East, we discover another practice related to the five elements. In Chinese medicine and spiritual philosophy, the five elements are Earth, Wood, Fire, Water, and Metal—Spirit is not part of this elemental mix. However, this system recognizes Spirit as the animating force that influences all five elements. In this system, Spirit is referred to as chi or qi.

In Ayurvedic medicine, we also see the practice of working with five elements. This tradition honors Air, Fire, Water, Earth, and Aether, or Akasha. Both Aether and Akasha are words for Spirit, and in older esoteric traditions the word Aether (or Ether) was used rather than Spirit.

These are just a handful of ways to look at Spirit in a spiritual context. It is by no means a simple conversation. Spirit is as Spirit does. Spirit is what you make of it. At the end of the day, you are your own spiritual authority, and how you relate, or don't relate, to Spirit is totally up to you.

Your mileage in a ritual context may vary. Honestly, that is what makes modern Witchcraft such a fascinating topic. There are many ways to approach magic and ritual. There isn't just *one true way* but rather lots of ways that help us connect to the larger spiritual world around us.

How to Use This Book

This book is a love letter to Spirit. Dip in and out of the pages and places that call to you. Flip through the book and perform bibliomancy to help you in your spiritual work. Let your Spirit guide you in your exploration of the world of Spirit. And if you want bonus Witch points, read the other books in this series—*Water Magic*, *Air Magic*, *Fire Magic*, and *Earth Magic*—to help you have a well-rounded approach to the elements in the world of the modern Witch.

Journal

If you have read enough books and followed their directions, you likely have dozens of journals, each dedicated to a specific training or book. This is something I have recommended in my other books. Having a journal for specific workings can help you to focus and have clarity on that topic. Plus, it helps you to look back at the work and remember. With this book, however, I don't suggest getting a brand-new journal. Instead, I simply encourage you to journal. When you have a *hit* on something, when a question pops into your head, or when anything comes up that might require more research or introspection, write that down in your journal.

And by *journal*, I mean that pretty blank-paged book that you bought for magical use, a Word document on your computer, your Notes app on your phone, or anything that you regularly check and read over. Journaling isn't just about writing down the thing; it's about going back to it and remembering it or reconnecting to it. Journaling is a way to reflect on your magic and your path as a spiritual being. So write down those interesting or curious things when they pop up, and they might open up a whole new world of Spirit.

Let's Begin

Exploring the elements is fundamental to a spiritual practice. It doesn't matter your level of experience, training, or the number of initiations you've had; connecting with the power of the elements will enhance any Witchcraft practice at any stage.

If you are new to magic, this book and the other books in this series will be a solid introduction to working with the unseen and seen realms magically. If you are an experienced practitioner, this book can help deepen your relationship to Spirit and the mystery that is all around us.

PART 1

HISTORY, FOLKLORE & MYTH

"I was born by myself but carry the spirit and blood of my father, mother, and my ancestors."

—Ziggy Marley

Chapter 1

SPIRIT THROUGHOUT TIME AND CULTURE

Spirit can be a lot of things, as noted in the introduction. Spirit can refer to the human soul, the energy of the land, the unknown or unseen, gods, and so much more. However, when we look at the word Spirit in relation to the word Aether, we can more easily follow the trail from ancient Western magical traditions to the practices of modern Witches.

Although the concepts of ghosts as spirits, the soul as a spirit, and the energy of ethereal beings that we might call spirit will come up in the chapters of this book, the goal here is to focus on Spirit as an element. In these pages we will address how Spirit shows up as an element and explore some of the practices and traditions connected to modern Witchcraft through the lens of that element.

Quintessence

A specific group of ancient peoples—whom we now refer to as medieval scientists but who could also easily be called Witches, alchemists, philosophers, or doctors—referred to Spirit as Aether or Quintessence. These were their terms for the material that exists beyond the earth. We might interpret this as relating to space or the solar system or even the larger universe, yet it is simultaneously much smaller than that. Aether pertains to concepts not fully understood by medieval scientists that which we now have names for, such as gravity, light, particles, cells, and sound waves.

Magic has always been connected to what is unexplainable.

Concepts that were once viewed as magic or Quintessence in the past have since been given names, descriptions, and explanations by modern science. However, just because something has a name and a definition doesn't change the fact that it is magical and mysterious. We might understand gravity as a scientific principle, but most of us don't grok the full depth of what gravity means and what it does. We get it because we experience it, but many of us don't understand the mathematics and science of how it works—and the good news is we don't need to. As with magic, we don't need to understand how gravity, light, or sound work to know that these things exist.

But science is only one part of how we look at the concept of Spirit. We can also see the impact of Spirit in the realms of sociology, philosophy, and history.

Ancient Greece

In ancient Greece, sometime between 750 and 650 BCE, Aether was viewed as the very air that the gods breathed, meaning it was charmed and full of mystery, literally the gods' breath, which is quite a magical idea. Anything we humans didn't yet understand or have language for would fall into the category of the gods' breath. The famous Greek writer Homer described Aether as pure, fresh air and clear sky.[1]

1 DeLay, "The Life and Death of the Aether (Part I)."

In the fourth century BCE, Plato wrote about the classical elemental system and the four elements of Air, Fire, Water, and Earth, but he also wrote of Aether as the "most translucent" of the elements. According to Plato, who was a student of Socrates, the four classical elements are stuck here on earth and exist only in connection to our planet. Spirit, or Aether, however, according to his worldview, is celestial and doesn't have any of the qualities you would find with the classical four because it isn't bound to the planet.

Aristotle, a student of Plato, further defined Aether in his treatise *On the Heavens.* In these works, he explained that Aether naturally moves in circular patterns and exhibits no unnatural motion. He noted that the movement of the planets and the solar system occurs in a circular fashion, implying that all celestial bodies are connected to the energy of Aether. He also referred to Aether as the primary matter.

Medieval Alchemy

Medieval alchemists, who practiced from the twelfth to the seventeenth centuries CE, also worked with Spirit, or Aether, but they called it Quintessence. Those who studied alchemy didn't believe that Quintessence had much of a presence on earth. Rather, they believed that the impact of Quintessence on our planet happened through how the other planets and celestial bodies impacted the earth.

During this time, medieval alchemists attempted to isolate, unravel, and understand the discipline that we now call astrology, believing this was part of the key to a deeper understanding of life and the universe. They wanted to gain power over healing and magic and thought the key to this was to harness Quintessence. These magicians wanted to use the pure energy of Quintessence to rid themselves of any impurities and become more powerful beings. The creation of the alchemists' famed philosopher's stone, which, once created, could offer never-ending life, required the use of Quintessence in the directions. As of now, no one has successfully created the philosopher's stone.

For the alchemist, connecting with Aether allowed the practitioner to enter a state of transcendence and receive divine intervention. In this view, Spirit connects the physical realm with the spiritual realm, allowing humans to connect to something greater than themselves.

Modern Science and Hermeticism

With the development of modern physics, many alchemical viewpoints on Aether and Quintessence slowly became scientifically obsolete. Yet the concept of Spirit, or Aether, never completely disappeared. Some modern physicists still use the term Quintessence to describe dark matter or dark energy. Although physicists believe dark matter exists, they can't explain how or why it works mathematically or scientifically. Quintessence in a modern scientific context still points to the potential of matter and energy.

Despite modern science's rejection of many ancient concepts, spiritual seekers—such as alchemists, hermeticists, and occultists—continued to discuss Quintessence as a metaphorical concept well into the 1900s.

For example, in his 1908 book *The Kybalion*, William Walker Atkinson shared his seven Hermetic principles, which speak to Quintessence as part of their esoteric viewpoint. These principles are considered major keys to self-empowerment in the occult and are still used and discussed in today's esoteric landscape.

The Hermetic principles create a spiritual structure in which you can manifest anything. These seven principles are as follows:

1. Principle of Mentalism—Everything that exists comes from the Divine Mind and we are part of that Divine Mind. There is no separation. Everything is part of one complex being. We are the dreamer and we are the dream.
2. Principle of Correspondence—"As above, so below." What happens in the spiritual realms will impact the physical and vice versa. All is connected and all will move to balance each other at all times.
3. Principle of Vibration—Everything in existence has a vibration, which means that everything is in a constant state of motion. We can connect and relate to anything by connecting with the vibration of that thing.
4. Principle of Polarity—All existence is connected by extremes or poles. All things are dual and the poles connect the extremes.
5. Principle of Rhythm—There is a natural ebb and flow to everything in the universe. It is subject to natural cycles.
6. Principle of Cause and Effect—Chance does not exist in the universe. Everything happens because something came into play to make it happen. Every moment that happens (effect) has a cause that brought it about.
7. Principle of Gender—Gender manifests in everything. The use of the word *gender* is outdated. This concept is actually about how all things have projective and receptive energies.

All these thought processes, dreams, explanations, and so forth just further lean into the fact that there are forces in this world that we can't fully understand. And we call these concepts Spirit, Aether, or Quintessence.

Modern Witchcraft

Modern practitioners of Witchcraft use some, all, or many of these ancient descriptors in their practices. In regard to Spirit and Witchcraft, Jaq D. Hawkins, author of *Elemental Spirits*, said, "It encompasses the basis for all of the other elements and is believed by magicians to be the fabric of existence through which magic transmits."[2] Spirit is the fabric through which magic transmits. This is really how it relates to what we do as modern practitioners.

One of the modern symbols connected to Spirit is the pentacle, a five-pointed star with a circle around it. This symbol shows the power of the five elements in unison. Earth, Air, Fire, Water, and Spirit all hold a point in the sacred star. Energy flows from one point to the next, creating the basis for magic in the universe.

The pentacle is a common symbol of power and protection in many modern Witchcraft practices. In many traditions, the pentacle is energetically used with a sacred knife called an *athame*, drawn at the four cardinal directions to create a magical container for rituals and spells.

2 Hawkins, *Elemental Spirits*, 22.

EXERCISE: The Word Quintessence

Speaking words is a form of magick. Allow Spirit to move through you with this activity. Find a time and place where you can be alone and undisturbed for at least thirty minutes. Allow yourself to get comfortable and relaxed. You should lie down or sit comfortably. Focus on your breath and allow your physical edges to feel like they are softening and expanding as you breathe. Let yourself breathe and open for a few minutes; don't rush this process. When you feel open and relaxed, focus on the word Quintessence. Simply repeat the word, either in your mind or out loud. Allow yourself to notice how it feels and what it brings up when you focus on it. Are there other words, images, sights, sounds, or feelings that come through as you meditate on this word? Repeat this process until you feel complete. When you are finished, write down anything odd or interesting that may have come up for you.

The Soul

We can't go deep into the concept of Spirit without taking into consideration the human soul. In many traditions, the terms Spirit and soul are used interchangeably. The soul, some might say, is the Spirit of the individual person. This is a modern Christian way of looking at the spiritual world. In this practice, the soul needs to seek salvation for eternity to be a positive experience and not endless torture.

The Nine-Part Soul of Ancient Egypt

In ancient Egypt, it was believed that the soul was made up of nine separate parts, each of which played an important role in life and the afterlife. Khat is the part of the soul that is the actual physical body. This part needs to be preserved for use in the afterlife. Ka is the astral body made up of the individual's personality. Ka is also the part of the soul that absorbs the energy from offerings left after death.

Ba is the spiritual force that can move between the body and the spirit realm. Shuyet is the shadow self, the shadow of Ka, or the astral body. Akh is the immortal self, the one that emerges when Ba and Ka are united.

Sahu is the ghost of the spirit. This is the part of the soul that can appear to others after the death of the individual. Sechem is the part of the soul that is enlightened and can help shift circumstances for the living from the afterlife. Ab is the heart, which is what defines an individual's character and needs to be preserved after death.

Finally, Ren is the secret name given by the gods at the time of birth. All these pieces make up the Spirit of a human being both in the physical realms and in the spiritual afterlife.[3]

The Triple Soul

Many of the ancient Greek philosophers believed there was a triple soul. The first part of the soul is the one that contains all the appetites. These are all the things a human craves: food, sex, pleasure, comforts, etc. The second part is the spirited part. This is the part of the soul that gets engaged, angry, or riled up. And finally, the third part of the soul is the mind. This is the part of the soul that is in charge. This part is rational and forward-thinking, what modern Jungian practitioners might consider the talking self.[4]

In some Eastern spiritual systems, such as Mahayana Buddhism and Jainism, there is a belief in a triple soul. One of these souls

3 Mark, "The Soul in Ancient Egypt."
4 Kerns, "Plato's Three Parts of the Soul."

stays with the body after death, one of the souls goes down into the underworld, and one of the souls goes up into heaven. Each soul serves its purpose for the individual, both in life and in the afterlife.[5]

If we look at modern spiritual practices, we find the triple soul in the Feri Tradition of modern Witchcraft. In the Feri Tradition, people have the talking self, which is the consciousness. This part of the soul is the one we hear in our heads. This voice is the director of our lives. The second part of the soul is called the fetch, which is the animal self or a child self. This part of the soul is wilder and more untamed, connected to the baser needs. Finally, the third part of the soul is the god-self, which could also be looked at as our superconsciousness. Each of these souls has a purpose, and when they align, we are performing at our best, for our highest good. Once again, we see the Spirit of the self not as just one thing, but as a relationship between various parts of being human.

Triple Realms

The concept of a triple soul lays perfectly on top of the idea that the world is made up of triple realms. One could argue that the realms of the world around us encompass the Spirit of where we live. If humans contain a triple soul, why wouldn't the universe also work within the bounds of a triple soul or Spirit?

The idea of the world being made up of triple realms is found in cultures worldwide. Many spiritual systems look at the world through a three-realm paradigm. In many of these systems, there is a central pole, tree, or axis that holds the world together.

In ancient Norse cosmology, the central pole of the multiverse is an ash tree called Yggdrasil. This world tree holds the three

5 Britannica, "Multiple Souls."

realms within it. The roots of the tree are the lower worlds, which are often a place of mystery, death, and regeneration. The realm of humans is the trunk of the tree, also called the middle world. At the top of the tree, the branches and leaves connect to the upper worlds, where the gods and mysterious ones reside.

In the *Poetic Edda*, an ancient collection of old Norse mythology, Odin hung from Yggdrasil for nine days and nine nights, which is how the tree got its name. Yggdrasil translates to "Odin's gallows" in Old Norse.

Yggdrasil is not only the frame that holds the world together, but also a living, breathing entity. Some creatures live in and among the trees. Some of these creatures cause harm to the roots or branches, while others share gossip between the different realms. The world tree is not immortal; it can be harmed. In this system of belief, the world, like the tree, will not live forever. It will come to an end at some point.

In Buddhist cosmology, there is a belief in a triple realm called Triloka. The lowest of these realms is the Desire realm, where humans live. The second is the Form realm, which is a physical realm that is separated from desire. The third realm is Formless, which is without desire or physicality.[6]

In shamanic practices, we see the three realms concept again. These are the Upper, Lower, and Middle Realms. The Upper Realms are etheric and spiritual. These are places beyond ego, where we can communicate with the gods and the spirits of higher vibration. The Lower Realms are connected to the deep. These are places of deep wisdom, earth, loam, and the darkness of the ocean.

6 Oxford Reference, "triloka."

Deep wisdom is in these realms. The Middle Realm is where we humans live. It is the world that we know.[7]

Modern Occultism

Spirit is also explored in the occult concept known as the Witches' Pyramid, which was first written about by Eliphas Levi in the early 1800s. Levi was a French occultist and author whose books are still popular in occult circles today. In his practice, to be a successful magician you had to adhere to the principles of the pyramid. The Witches' Pyramid sits on four corners made up of the classical elements, Air, Fire, Water, and Earth.[8]

The element of Air holds down one corner of the Witches' Pyramid. Air connects to the power "To Know." By understanding Air, we understand the energy of what it is to have knowledge. With this awareness, we know that learning is a continual process, a never-ending unfolding.

The element of Fire holds down the next corner of the pyramid. Fire is connected to the power of Will. When we understand the power of Fire, we understand our own personal will. This is an important key to magic. In our practice, our will must be stronger than the thing we are facing.

The next corner of the pyramid is associated with the element of Water, which is connected to the power "To Dare." What is more daring than water? Water is the flow of energy and movement, which shows us how to be daring in our magic. To dare means being brave enough to take action.

The final corner of the pyramid is anchored by the element of Earth, which teaches us the power of keeping silent. Magic occurs

7 Therapeutic Shamanism, "The Shamanic Journey: A Journey to the Three Shamanic Realms."

8 Mankey, "The Witches' Pyramid."

when we learn to remain quiet about it. Once upon a time, keeping silent could have even been a matter of life and death in the practice of Witchcraft. In modern times, our magic can be diluted when shared before it is fully developed.

The power of the Witches' Pyramid rests on the four corners of Air, Fire, Water, and Earth, but when they are combined, they create the point at the top. This pinnacle of the pyramid is where we direct our magic. Some groups call this point "To Go" or "To Go into the World." It is at this point that the power of Spirit comes into play. Spirit moves the energy of the elements into the realm of magic and manifestation.

Wicca

Wicca and many traditions that have branched off from Wicca acknowledge only the four elements in their ritual structure. Spirit is seen as the animating force that moves in and between the other elements. In the Wiccan ritual format, there is a spoken acknowledgment to Air, Fire, Water, and Earth, while the center of the circle is acknowledged silently. It is the center of the circle and not the element of Spirit.

Conclusion

The way people have viewed and worked with Spirit over the centuries has changed and evolved. Spirit can show us how much science, technology, and magic have in common. Whether we call it Aether, Quintessence, black matter, or Spirit, we know there is a lot out there that we don't understand. That's what Spirit is all about.

Chapter 2

MYTHOLOGICAL SPIRIT BEASTS AND PLACES

Any beast or place that is mythological could be connected to the element of Spirit just due to the fact that it is mythological! Myth comes to us from the realms of the mythopoetic and speaks to something deep within our humanity. Myth, like story, is part of the subconscious that all human beings can draw from. As such, mythology itself is rooted in the realm of Spirit.

Mythological Spirit beasts and places help us remember that we are connected to higher planes of existence and are spiritual beings having a human experience.

Mythical Beasts

Beings that are otherworldly, tricksters, psychopomps, connected to dreamtime, or shape-shifters all hold a bit of the ineffable energy that is so much Spirit-based. These are the beings that can show you how to be spiritual, travel between the realms, and stay outside of what is considered the norm. The following Spirit beasts are from all corners of the globe. They are the beings to seek out when you don't know what else to do.

Anansi

This trickster spirit, sometimes considered a god, comes from West Africa, and his stories exist throughout the African diaspora into the Caribbean, South America, and the United States. Although this creature is often seen as a spider, he is known to be able to shape-shift into other beings, including humans. Anansi is known for putting his own needs first, which often leads to creating chaos for humans and the other gods alike. He is also known to go between the worlds helping humans communicate with the other deities. In modern practices, Anansi is seen as an entity of wit and storytelling. Although he is a trickster, he often brings you the lessons of your creation through his trickery. What you sow, he will help you reap. This is often done in a playful and comedic way. He can triumph over opponents who have more strength than he does, which speaks very much to those who suffered under enslavement and have cultural origins with this being.[9]

Angel

Angels are creatures beyond form that come from Christianity, Zoroastrianism, Hinduism, and Judaism. The Bible states that angels were created before the material universe. They are known as messengers or intermediaries for greater forms of divinity, the most well-known being the angels that serve as messengers between the Christian God and humans. These beings are connected to good energy, protection, and guiding forces. In the Judaic system, angels exist in a hierarchy, with different angels having dominion over lesser ones according to their rank. Angels are often depicted as looking human, but many of them are quite

9 Prabhu, *The Compendium of Mythical Creatures*, 47–50.

terrifying. Sometimes they are shaped like burning wheels, having many eyes, or creatures with many wings and many eyes.

Aswang

In Filipino folklore, the Aswang are shape-shifting beings who are known to wreak havoc on humans. They move about during the night and have a taste for human flesh. However, as many stories as there are about them eating humans, there are just as many about them healing humans, curing diseases, or removing curses. As shape-shifters, the Aswang can take on the appearance of anything they want, including humans. Although they can look like anything or anyone, what gives them away is their sharp teeth and glowing eyes. They are known to come out only at night.

Baku

The Baku originated in Shintoism in Japan. They can ward off negative energy and bring good fortune. They are known to eat nightmares and are called upon to help alleviate bad dreams. Pictures of them are often found in the bedrooms of those suffering from nightmares. They have a rather odd appearance, with the body of a bear, the trunk of an elephant, the tail of an ox, and the legs of a tiger.[10]

Banshee

Banshees come from Irish and Celtic folklore. It is believed that if you hear the wail of a banshee, it is a message of impending death. Banshees are always seen as female figures. Sometimes they are scary and grotesque, sometimes they are more ethereal, and sometimes they are beautiful and sad. They can be old or young, but the one constant is the sound they make. The wail of a banshee

10 Prabhu, *The Compendium of Mythical Creatures*, 86–87.

is a terrifying keening sound. Most of the folklore surrounding the banshee describes them as neutral beings. They only keen for those about to die, but they aren't the ones that mark that individual for death. In other folk beliefs, each family has their own banshee, and she only cries before one of the family members is about to die.[11]

Demon

Demons are the opposite of angels in Christian mythology. They are the negative entities that serve as emissaries of the devil or Satan. Depending on the tradition and system of beliefs, demons could simply be evil or malevolent spirits or they could be angels that fell from heaven. Like angels, demons are noncorporeal and may take on many forms, including animals or hybrids, or they can look like humans.

Domovoi

The domovoi come to us from Slavic cultures. They are the house spirits that look over the home and the people who live there. These beings are described as small men with long, shaggy hair and beards. The folk belief is the more hair they have, the happier the home they inhabit. The domovoi have bright eyes and bare feet and are known to shape-shift. They could appear in your home as a small animal, such as a frog, cat, or snake. However, they are also known to be shy, so they often keep themselves invisible. Although you might not be able to see them, you can hear them running through the house. They like animals and small children and will often allow themselves to be seen by them. They are the guardians of the Spirit of the home, so treating them with respect and honor is important.[12]

11 Prabhu, *The Compendium of Mythical Creatures*, 93–95.

12 Pamita, *Baba Yaga's Book of Witchcraft*, 31–43.

Enenra

In Japanese folklore, the enenra are beings of smoke. They are formless and shapeless, able to move as the smoke moves. They are known to cause harm to humans, especially those who are vulnerable, and can only be stopped with water. Some believe the enenra are the smoke that carries souls of the dead.[13]

Incubus/Succubus

The incubus and succubus are demons who visit unsuspecting humans while they sleep and engage in sexual activities with them. In folklore, the incubus is male and seeks out women, while the succubus is female and seeks out men. Along with engaging in sexual activity, the succubus will steal a man's seed to create more demons. The origins of the incubus and succubus aren't certain. They show up in Jewish mythology, Islamic folklore, and other stories and myths from the Middle East. Both incubus and succubus operate in dreams, the realm of Spirit communication. They are often blamed for sleep paralysis, where an individual wakes up but cannot move or speak. In these cases, it is believed that a demon, in this case an incubus or a succubus, is lying or sitting on top of the person, which is why they cannot move or speak. Sometimes this phenomenon is called being *hag-ridden*.[14]

Kikimora

The kikimora is found in Slavic folklore. These are helpful spirits who do chores around the house but are also known for being mischievous and playing pranks. Their temperament is often linked to the temperament of the people who live in the home where the kikimora is found. If the humans are mean and angry, then

13 Prabhu, *The Compendium of Mythical Creatures*, 271.

14 Prabhu, *The Compendium of Mythical Creatures*, 397–99, 539–41.

the kikimora will be too. The kikimora is often seen as the female counterpart of the domovoi. They are odd-looking creatures. They are very small and hunchbacked, with long noses and hairy bodies. If they feel disrespected, they can create a lot of chaos. By leaving them offerings, you can stay in their good graces.[15]

Kurgarra and Galatur

In Sumerian mythology, the god Enki picked dirt out of his nails and created the Kurgarra and Galatur. They are two little beings without gender who are able to travel to the underworld without being seen. Enki made them to save his niece Inanna from being kept in the underworld forever. In the mythology of Inanna, Kurgarra and Galatur are described as fly-like creatures, asexual, genderless, and small. Because they showed empathy to Ereshkigal, they were able to save the life of the goddess Inanna.

Sphinx

From Egyptian, Persian, and Greek myth and legend come the stories and iconography of the sphinx. Sphinxes are depicted as having a lion's body with a human head and face. Occasionally they are also depicted with wings, breasts, and a tail. The sphinx is believed to be a guardian spirit, protecting an area or region. To get past the sphinx, you need to answer its riddles. If the riddles are answered incorrectly, the sphinx will devour the human seeking passage. In some legends the sphinx is omniscient, being able to see and know all.

Spirits of Place

Spirits of place are beings, and at the same time they are more than beings. Ultimately, spirits of place are the energies, entities,

15 Prabhu, *The Compendium of Mythical Creatures*, 429–30.

and/or beings that live in specific locations. This concept comes from the ancient Roman idea of the *genius loci.* All locations have a spirit and a unique energy signature. We humans can interact and work with these spirits. These energies are often neutral beings born of the events that happened in that specific location. A place that has held a lot of trauma might feel haunted, while a sacred site that has witnessed a lot of worship and love may feel like a place of blessings and love. Spirits of place are also an animistic way of looking at the world. All things—rocks, plants, trees, streets, crosswalks, etc.—have an inherent spirit.

Titans

The Titans come from ancient Greek culture and were forces of nature. They didn't embody or represent the energy of the elements; rather, they *were* the elements. They were then contained and conquered by the head of the Olympians, Zeus. Through this transition from the ancient Greeks being ruled by forces of nature to one single sky god, we can see the culture of ancient Greece become more of a patriarchal society.

Valkyries

The Valkyries come from Norse mythology. They are the beings that sweep the battlefield and collect the best of the fallen warriors, taking them to Valhalla to train for the final battle at the end of the world. The Valkyries are all beautiful and powerful women who wear headdresses with wings on them and are excellent warriors in their own right. They are often seen on the backs of horses, boars, or wolves, carrying weapons to the battlefield. They are often referred to as the handmaidens of Odin. The Valkyries are the psychopomps of war, helping the dead move from one realm to the next.[16]

Will-o'-the-Wisp

These beings come from folklore in the Celtic diaspora and Western Europe. They are beings of light, often called ghostlight, that form over marshes or swamps. Following the light of a will-o'-the-wisp often leads to being lost or falling into the marshes. The lights are bluish in color and float along the landscape. These lights do not flicker like a flame but are steady. Depending on the region and folklore, these beings could be fae, the dead, or even a scientific phenomenon. Some even say they are small pixie-like beings that carry small lights with them to lure people into danger.[17]

Mythical Places

Locations that are known to be gateways or openings to other realms are Spirit-marked places. These places could be legendary or they could be local. You likely live near a place that has been marked by Spirit or has the energy of Spirit. Mythological Spirit places can be seen in the realms of the "otherworlds," where the dead or the fae belong. These places are often just next to the human realms.

Annwn

Annwn is the underworld in Welsh and Celtic mythology. The word Annwn translated into English means non-world, within a world, and/or very deep. In most stories Annwn is located in the deep, either underground, under sacred sites, or in the deep water. However, this realm is located right next to the realm of humans.

16 Prabhu, *The Compendium of Mythical Creatures*, 563–65.
17 Prabhu, *The Compendium of Mythical Creatures*, 581–82.

Some myth alludes to the dead being in this location, but it is also home to fae beings and the gods of Welsh myth.

Avalon

Avalon is the mythical resting place of King Arthur and is the location of many priestesses guarding the otherworld. Avalon is a mythical island, but it could have roots in a physical location in the United Kingdom. Many believe the town of Glastonbury is the modern site of the mythical Avalon. Some say that Avalon is not of the human realm but is separated from us by a veil of magic. This magic may simply be of the otherworld or may have been put into place by the priestesses of the holy island.

Axis Mundi

The term *axis mundi* is Latin in origin. The axis mundi is where heaven meets earth; it is the line or the "stem" that runs through the planet's center. It is the world tree, the pole and center of the universe that holds everything together. Although the term is Latin, the concept can be found in practices from China, Japan, ancient Greece, Mayan mythology, Hinduism, Buddhism, the Old Testament, and Sioux traditions, just to name a few.[18] Each culture has its own name for this central point, but the universal term is axis mundi.

Duat

The underworld in Egyptian mythos is a land called Duat, although some translate this world to mean the afterlife. In the Egyptian system, the human spirit must travel through Duat to make it to the final stage of the afterlife after death. The final stage of Duat is what modern folks might consider "heaven." But to

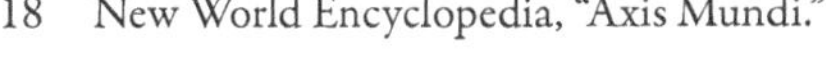

18 New World Encyclopedia, "Axis Mundi."

reach this final stage, the spirit must successfully navigate arduous challenges, landscapes, and beings that can cause harm, including completely devouring the soul. Each person was provided a book of the dead when they were entombed in order to help them navigate the perils of Duat.[19]

Elysium

In ancient Greek culture, Elysium was the place of paradise that only certain people would go to after death. According to ancient Greek beliefs, the afterlife, also called the underworld or Hades, was filled with different realms. Each of these realms offered something different to the souls that arrived there. Some of these places were lovely and comfortable and some were scary and torturous. Elysium is the realm where heroes, gods, and the lucky chosen few will go. The belief in Elysium likely comes from the older Minoan culture originally. Some ancient writers referred to this place as a land of perfect happiness or the Isle of the Blessed.

Fountain of Youth

The Fountain of Youth is a mythological place with stories found in many different cultures. It is believed that drinking from the fountain will bestow everlasting youth and, in some versions of the mythology, immortality. Numerous modern locations claim to be the site of the true Fountain of Youth; however, no one has yet received the blessing of everlasting youth from any of these places—or, if they have, they aren't discussing it. The Fountain of Youth was first mentioned in the fifth century by Herodotus. This myth expanded during the Crusades and grew even more during the sixteenth century, during the Age of Exploration, which I like to refer to as the Age of Pirates. This includes a site in St. Augus-

19 Naydler, *Temple of the Cosmos*, 126.

tine, Florida, established by the Spanish when they arrived on the North American continent.

Heaven

Heaven is the mythological place in Christian belief where souls go after death. Of course, the catch is that one must be a good person or have undergone specific rituals or blessings to be counted among those who get to enter heaven. The rules for entering heaven vary depending on the particular denomination of Christianity. This celestial realm is filled with clouds, music, and positive energy. In some traditions, it is also the realm where angels reside when they are not assisting humans on earth.

KunLun Mountains

The KunLun Mountains are a range in Asia. These mountains are said to be one of the most inhospitable places for humans on the planet. In the Taoist traditions, this mountain range is where the gods reside. It is also the location of the axis mundi, or the central pole of the world, in this system of belief. Although the KunLun mountain range literally exists, it is a place filled with myth and legend and is said to be paradise.[20]

The Underworld

The concept of the underworld appears in cultures across the globe, including the ancient Greeks, Egyptians, Celts, Aztecs, Buddhists, Jewish mythology, and Christian mythology. Each culture has its own ideas, images, and myths regarding what the underworld looks like and the journey to reach it. Generally speaking, across virtually all traditions, the underworld is a place where souls go after death. This could be a realm of abundance and

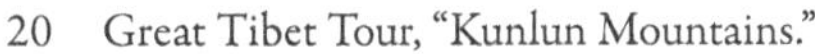

20 Great Tibet Tour, "Kunlun Mountains."

beauty, a land with various realms and destinations, a domain of ethereal beings, or a location of punishment. It varies by culture.

Valhalla

In ancient Norse mythology, Valhalla is the place where the chosen dead go after they have died a good death. A "good death" means a warrior's death that would make their warrior ancestors proud. The Valkyries must specifically choose which fallen warriors are allowed to enter Valhalla. However, Valhalla is not a place of rest. The warriors brought to this realm are expected to train for the final battle in Norse mythology, called Ragnarök.

Watchtowers

The concept of Watchtowers originated in Enochian magic, a system developed during the Renaissance by John Dee and Edward Kelley. Centuries later, these spiritual ideas were adopted by practitioners of the Golden Dawn spiritual order. Through the practices of this fraternal order, the Watchtowers found their way into modern Wicca and many contemporary traditions of Witchcraft. According to myth, there is a spiritual "Watchtower" in each corner of the planet, located in the four cardinal directions: east, south, west, and north. Each Watchtower contains an angelic spirit that rules its realm and corresponds to a specific element. The realm of Air is in the east, Fire in the south, Water in the west, and Earth in the north.

Yggdrasil

In ancient Norse mythology, the central point or pole of the world is a tree called Yggdrasil. In this cosmology, there are nine realms, and the world tree holds them together. Yggdrasil is a massive ash tree that is most often connected with stories of the god

Odin. Some creatures and animals live in and around the tree, and they all have an impact on the realms in some way, shape, or form.

Conclusion

Spirit is magic. When it comes to mythological beasts and places, of course we are going to find Spirit there. Even if we were to look at these creatures and locations through the lens of the four other elements, we would still be able to see the thread of Spirit moving through them all. The realms of Spirit are also the places where our spirit goes after death. Spirit is the mystery and the unknown.

Chapter 3

SPIRIT AND THE DIVINE

One could say that all the Divine is connected to Spirit. The Divine does not exist without Spirit; in many ways, the Divine *is* Spirit. As the introduction notes, many modern Witchcraft traditions acknowledge only the four elements in their rituals and ceremonies. These traditions don't specifically name Spirit in that context, but they will call down or invoke deities in their rituals and circles.

Deities that stand outside of time and space or rule over all the elements are those more specifically connected to the realm of Spirit. Remember, your mileage may vary when it comes to the realm of Spirit and magic. What feels like an entity of a specific element to you could be connected to a different element for another practitioner. There isn't one simple answer. Divinity is more complex than that.

The deities of Spirit exist in the liminal places. A liminal space isn't this nor that; it is both and neither. These are the beings of between places. Deities of Spirit are also creators and helped bring the world into being. Spirit deities are not gods connected to specific jobs, elements, or energy, but they are primordial. The deities of Spirit are also those who can travel between the realms. They are not bound to one part of existence but can move between them.

The most important writing about the Divine from a modern Witchcraft perspective is the Charge of the Goddess by Doreen Valiente. This is a beautiful piece of poetry that many Witchcraft traditions use in their practices. It has been altered and rewritten many times over the years by other Witchcraft practitioners, but the original still holds up to the beauty.

Very few things connect different Witchcraft traditions together, but the Charge of the Goddess feels like it represents the spirit of modern Witchcraft. It is a piece of poetry that unifies and connects many different practices and practitioners. Because it is a poem written as if the Goddess herself wrote it, it is a piece of modern myth for modern Witches. One of my favorite parts is at the very end of the Charge:

> [I]f that which thou seekest thou findest not within thee, thou wilt never find it without thee. For behold, I have been with thee from the beginning; and I am that which is attained at the end of desire.[21]

The Deities

The following list of deities can help show you different ways to relate to Spirit. They come from different regions and cultures, but they all shine some wisdom on that elusive thing we call Spirit.

Aether

In the ancient Greek pantheon, Aether is the primordial god of heaven and light. You might recognize this word from the beginning of the book when we discussed other words for Spirit, Aether

21 This version of the Charge appears in *A Witches' Bible* by Janet and Stewart Farrar, 43.

being one of them! He exists between the dome of air above us and the earthbound mists. He overthrew his parents, Erebos (darkness) and Nyx (night), to take control of light and space. Aether is described as a human personification of light, glowing with blond hair and brown skin.[22]

Brahma

In the Hindu religion, Brahma is one of the creator gods. He is the primeval first god of the Hindu pantheon. He is the creator, having made everything on earth and all living creatures here. He is pictured with four heads looking in each direction and is connected to the primordial energy of creation.[23]

Cacoch

In the Mayan spiritual system, Cacoch is the creator god. He created a water lily, and from this plant all the rest of the Mayan pantheon was born. In Mayan iconography, Cacoch looks like a typical Mayan man, meaning you wouldn't know he was a god if he was in front of you. He is unassuming and could look like anyone.[24]

Charon

In ancient Greek mythology, Charon is a psychopomp. He is the ferryman who takes people from the realm of the living to the realm of the dead. Charon is described as unkempt, with a long beard and tattered robes. He pushes the ferry along the river Styx with a long pole and doesn't speak to those he ferries.

22 Jordan, *Encyclopedia of Gods*, 6.
23 Jordan, *Encyclopedia of Gods*, 46.
24 Jordan, *Encyclopedia of Gods*, 50.

Daimons

If you were to look up the definition of this word, you would find that it translates to *demon* in English, but that isn't exactly correct. In ancient Greek culture, a daimon was a spiritual being attached to each human. This spirit is a part of each person's fundamental character. Each daimon has a unique appearance, as does each human being.

Es

Es, the creator god, comes from the Siberian area. He is known to be an old man with a black beard. He made the first humans out of clay. As he walked, he tossed these clay beings behind him. Those tossed behind him from his right hand became men and those from his left hand became women.[25]

Euphrosyne

In ancient Greece, the goddess Aphrodite had attendant spirits called the Charities. Euphrosyne is one of these beings, known for bringing joy and good feelings. She helps fill the world with happy moments. She is depicted as a beautiful young woman in the prime of her life.

Ganesha

In the Hindu system, Ganesh (or Ganesha) is known as the deity of art and wisdom and the remover of obstacles. With an elephant head and human body, Ganesh is the son of Shiva. He is so beloved that he is worshiped in the temples of other gods and is a common household deity.[26]

25 Jordan, *Encyclopedia of Gods*, 79.
26 Jordan, *Encyclopedia of Gods*, 86.

Gwyn ap Nudd

This underworld god originates in Celtic and Welsh traditions. He is known for leading hunts and ruling over the realm called Annwn. It is believed that Gwyn ap Nudd emerges from the ground in sacred places, such as Glastonbury in the United Kingdom. He is depicted cloaked, with a darkened face, guiding a pack of white dogs. The white dogs often have red or pink ears. In this mythology, creatures from the otherworld are frequently white with red or pink ears.[27]

Hecate

In ancient Greece, Hecate was considered a goddess of the crossroads and liminal spaces. There aren't a lot of shrines and temples that remain for this deity because she was a protector of those liminal places and shrines existed for her in every home. In modern times, she has evolved into a goddess of Witches. In ancient myth, she was able to go between the realms. She was one of the deities who brokered a deal between Hades, Persephone, and Demeter. Hecate has been pictured in many different ways. Sometimes she is seen as a young and beautiful woman and other times as a haggard crone. She is sometimes seen with three heads and/or several animal heads.[28]

Heimdall

In ancient Norse mythology, Heimdall was a god of liminal spaces. He guarded over the Bifrost, which is a gate that connects different realms together, making it possible to move between the worlds. Heimdall is known as a great guardian because he does not sleep and can see in the darkness. In the myths, Heimdall is

27 Jordan, *Encyclopedia of Gods*, 91.
28 Jordan, *Encyclopedia of Gods*, 99–100.

described as good-looking, with bright, glowing white skin and gold teeth. He is described as having a long beard and carrying a horn.[29]

Horus

In the ancient Egyptian system, Horus was the son of Isis and Osiris, created after Osiris was resurrected through a magickal insemination ritual. Horus is the sun and the morning star and is believed to be the energy of Quintessence. Horus is a falcon-headed man with a red and white crown and is also depicted as a full falcon. One of his eyes is the sun and the other is the morning star.[30]

Hyperion

In ancient Greece, Hyperion was one of the Titans. He was the god of primordial light, ruler of the east and the dawn. There aren't many descriptions of Hyperion or the Titans in general. As a Titan, Hyperion was made up of glowing light, literally being the dawn.[31]

Janus

In ancient Rome, Janus was the deity of liminality. He has two faces, one looking forward and one looking backward. He watches over doorways, gates, entryways, and so forth. He is sometimes called the god of all beginnings. He is often seen with keys so that he can open doorways.[32]

Legba

In the West African and African diaspora traditions, Legba, also known as Papa Legba, is a psychopomp. He is the intermedi-

29 Jordan, *Encyclopedia of Gods*, 99.
30 Jordan, *Encyclopedia of Gods*, 107.
31 Jordan, *Encyclopedia of Gods*, 110.
32 Jordan, *Encyclopedia of Gods*, 124.

ary between humans and all the other deities. In order to connect with any of the African gods, you must first go through him. As a trickster deity, Legba is depicted in many different ways. Sometimes he is an older man in tattered clothes, walking with dogs and a walking stick. He is often seen with a wide-brimmed hat, smoking a pipe.[33]

Math ap Mathonwy

In ancient Welsh mythology, Math ap Mathonwy is a deity of magic. His story is found in the *Mabinogion*, a collection of Welsh folktales. He is a powerful magician; in fact, in the myths he is referred to as the most powerful magician of his time. However, there are no descriptions of what he might have looked like.

Melinoe

In the ancient Greek pantheon, Melinoe is a goddess of nightmares. She is from the underworld and is connected to ghosts. As the daughter of Hades and Persephone, Melinoe is said to be dark on one side and light on the other, based on the energy of her parents. She is also described as flowy or ghostly.

Mercury/Hermes

In ancient Rome, Mercury was a psychopomp. Also known as Hermes in Greece, this deity can go between the worlds. He is the messenger of the gods and helps the gods and humans communicate with each other. He is known to bring good fortune and has been known to help all kinds of gods and mortals. As a psychopomp, he leads the dead into the underworld. He was depicted as an attractive beardless youth wearing a helmet with wings. He also had wings around his feet, helping him move between the realms.[34]

33 Jordan, *Encyclopedia of Gods*, 144.
34 Jordan, *Encyclopedia of Gods*, 163.

Neith

The ancient Egyptian creator goddess is called Neith. She emerged from the primordial ocean and followed the flow of the Nile River in Egypt. Neith birthed the cosmos and the gods and is recognized as the mother of all Egyptian rulers. She is depicted as a powerful woman donning a red crown and wielding a bow and arrows.[35]

The Norns

In the ancient Norse mythology system, the Norns are made up of three entities: Urd, Verdandi, and Skuld. They represent the powers of past, present, and wyrd, respectively. Wyrd isn't "the future," but rather is the word for possibility. The Norns are neutral, neither good nor bad. They are seen as three old women with gray hair. They live in the roots of the world tree, Yggdrasil.

Star Goddess

In the Feri Tradition of Witchcraft, there is an origin myth featuring a spirit called the Star Goddess. She is literally the primordial reaches of space. In the myth, she gazes upon her reflection in the dark mirror of space and falls in love. From that moment of love, she gives birth to the universe. She is depicted as the Milky Way.

Tai Yi

Tai Yi is the ancient Chinese god who was the spirit of the universe before anything else was created. He was the only thing before there was anything. He is embodied in the Pole Star. He has been depicted as a strange being with antlers.[36]

35 Jordan, *Encyclopedia of Gods*, 180.
36 Jordan, *Encyclopedia of Gods*, 249.

Tiamat

This goddess comes from the Mesopotamian regions. Tiamat is the primordial goddess existing in the depths of the waters. Her eyes became the source of the Tigris. Tiamat is sometimes described as a human woman, or a body of water, or a woman and dragon hybrid.[37]

Spirit Guides

We should also remember our personal spirit guides in the realm of Spirit magic. Each of us has our own personal pantheon, potentially made up of deities, ancestors, angels, spirits of the land, and numerous other unseen beings. These guides are unique to each of us and serve as guiding forces and protectors throughout our lives. Discovering some of your personal spirit guides and developing relationships with them is possible, making communication easier.

Animal Allies

Animal allies can take several forms. An animal could be a physical creature you have a relationship with, a beloved pet, an animal you admire, or one that resonates with you. These allies can assist our spiritual work while they are alive and even after they have passed on. See more about animal allies and working with animals of Spirit in chapter 8.

Ancestral Allies

A spiritual ancestral ally is a guardian spirit from one of your own ancestral lineages. This could be someone of your blood and ancestry or someone of spirit. When it comes to blood ancestors, there is an ease in communication because your ancestors' blood is literally flowing in your veins. It doesn't matter what you know

37 Jordan, *Encyclopedia of Gods*, 260.

about your ancestors. It doesn't matter if you are adopted or uncertain about who your ancestors are. They are still in your blood and bones, and you can use that connection to develop a relationship with them.

Guardian Spirits

I'm using the term guardian spirits as a catch-all for the beings that may serve as our allies and might not fall into the other categories. These beings could be fae allies, angels, spirits of your home or land, or familiar spirits that have walked with others in your family. These beings don't exist in the world as humans do and likely have never had a corporeal existence on the earth. These beings likely don't have a good grasp of the rules of what it is to be human and may cause chaos or issues because they don't understand human rules.

Mighty Ones

The Mighty Ones, sometimes referred to as the Mighty Ones of the Craft, are the ancestors of our Witchcraft traditions and lineages. These spirits were one real people, both known and unknown, who passed on their wisdom and understanding of magic. A Mighty One could be a spiritual ancestor from your lineage of Witchcraft or a well-known historical figure, such as Doreen Valiente.

Plant Allies

Plant allies are those spiritual beings that come in the form of green bloods, plants, trees, botanicals, and the like. See more on working with Spirit plants in chapter 6.

Working with Spirit Guides

One of the easiest ways to start working with your spirit guides is to allow yourself to be open to the process. Learning to discern your voice from the voices of any of your spiritual allies takes some time. There is a strong likelihood that you have several spiritual guides or allies that walk with you on a daily basis. The point is to start listening for them and working with them.

To keep it simple, it's best to begin by seeking a connection with one of your allies. Ancestral allies are a great starting point, especially if you feel overwhelmed about where to start. Ancestors are part of your physical makeup, meaning they are connected to your body, and thus are easier to form a relationship with.

Relationships with spirit guides may be lifelong, or an ally may come into your life for a specific reason.

When you first open up to your allies, make time and space for communication. This can be done at an altar or really anywhere. Each day, speak to the ally you want to work with and then sit in silence to wait for a response. Initially it's likely that nothing will happen, but stick with it and continue this practice every day. Over time you will begin to receive communication from your ally.

Communication with a spirit guide could look like a sign or symbol. It could be a specific animal that shows up every time you sit in meditation, or there could be a word, noise, scent, or feeling that you experience. It could be that you hear a voice or receive a message. You could get a feeling or hear a whisper. At the start, the messages that come through will often be subtle, so pay attention to the signs.

However, after time, the messages will become clearer and more obvious. As you learn to hear the voice of your ally and discern the difference between their voice and yours, communication between the two of you will become easier. Then you will be able to hear what kind of offerings they may want or know what signs or symbols they will send when they need or want your attention. The relationship will build, just like a relationship with another human might.

EXERCISE: Journey to the Spirit Temple

To find a Spirit ally, you can visit the Spirit temple as a way to start the journey. This exercise is a guided meditation or trance. You can either have someone read this meditation to you or record it and play it back. When reading a trance out loud, remember to read slowly and leave space for the experience to unfold. This meditation can be repeated over and over again if you want to meet more allies, but be cautious about doing this too many times and overwhelming yourself with allies. It's best to do it once and focus on getting to know that ally. Let that relationship unfold and build. Once you feel firm and solid in that relationship, then you might consider doing this process again.

Needs

At least thirty minutes of uninterrupted time
Journal and pen
Glass of water

The Journey

Allow yourself to get comfortable and begin to relax. Take some long, slow breaths, and as you do, allow your edges to soften and expand. With each inhale and exhale, let yourself fall deeper and deeper into a place of relaxation. (*Pause here.*)

With each breath, let yourself soften more and more. From this place of expansion, allow your Witch's eye to open. Your Witch's eye is that all-seeing eye that sits above and between your normal seeing eyes. Let that all-seeing eye open up.

When your Witch's eye is open, you see before you a pathway. Let yourself begin to follow this path. Place one foot in front of the other and continue to move forward on this path. As you walk, notice the landscape around you. Notice if there are any interesting plants or animals that may exist along the pathway. As you move along this path, step-by-step, you notice ahead of you a bend in the path.

As you reach this bend, you see before you an opening in the path, a widening and broadening. In the middle of this opening is your Spirit Temple. (*Pause here.*)

Notice the details of this temple. What is the size and shape of this place? What does it look and feel like? Take in the specifics of this temple, as it is here just for you and only you. Pay attention to the area that surrounds your temple and anything else interesting that stands out to you about this place. (*Pause here.*)

All your spiritual allies can be met within this magical temple. Remember that today you are here to meet with just one of these allies, but you can return any time to meet again with this ally or to connect with others.

As you approach the Spirit Temple, one of your spiritual allies comes out to meet you. This ally may walk on many feet, or float, or fly. This ally may swim, or slither, or move in some way totally unfamiliar to you. (*Pause here.*)

Allow this ally to fully come into form as you approach it. Visually take in the full display of your ally. When you feel ready, talk with this ally. See what information it has for you today and see if it will tell you its name. (*Pause here.*)

Take a moment to ask any other questions that are on your mind for this ally. (*Pause here.*)

When you feel ready, ask your ally for a sign or symbol so you will know when it wants to connect with you. (*Pause here.*)

Again, our time in this place is limited, but you can return here at any time. Take a moment to thank your ally and offer gratitude for this experience. (*Pause here.*)

When you are ready, turn away from your Spirit Temple and begin to follow the path that brought you here. With one foot in front of the other, you follow the path, step-by-step, back the way you came. Continue along the path and notice if anything looks different from when you entered this place.

As you follow this path, notice how your Witch's eye begins to close back down to its normal state of being. Allow your Witch's eye to close back down, and as it does, become aware of your body. (*Pause here.*)

Take some deep breaths and notice how it feels to be in your body right now. Breathe and connect in with your edges. Allow the edges of your body to firm up around you, returning to their normal state of being. Breathe in and fully come back into your body. Slowly open your eyes and notice the space around you.

Allow yourself to slowly get up and move around. Write down anything you want to remember from this event. Drink a glass of water to help you fully come back into your body.

Conclusion

In many ways, the element of Spirit allows us to access the realm of the gods more easily. Spirit is the element that links humans and other beings together. Through the realm of Spirit, we can most easily connect to mystery. The Divine and humanity have Spirit in common.

The most important aspect of understanding Spirit and the Divine is to remember that you are your own spiritual authority. In the Reclaiming Tradition of Witchcraft, there is a saying: "You are your own spiritual authority, rooted in community." This means you get to define what is right for your own spiritual practice; there is no intermediary between you and the gods—or the Divine. The idea of being rooted in community emphasizes that our personal practices should not affect or interfere with another practitioner's beliefs and practices.

Chapter 4

SACRED SPIRIT SITES

Sacred Spirit sites exist all over the world. Some of them are loud and big and obvious, like the Grand Canyon in Arizona, while others are quiet and subtle, like the seasonal creek that shows up in your neighborhood. Some of these Spirit places are famous and well-known, such as Stonehenge. However, the best and most important sacred Spirit sites are the ones that are local to you and may not be famous or even known to anyone else, such as the Ashokawna River, commonly known as the Russian River, here in the town where I live.

As Witches and Pagans, we have a responsibility to the land we inhabit. No matter where you go in the world, you will find places where the veil feels thin, as if you are stepping into a supernatural realm. A thin place may feel magical or sacred, even without a marker or explanation. These locations could be in your local park or on your route to work. They might whisper to you when you visit. Entering a sacred site can make the hairs on the back of your neck stand up or give you goose bumps as you walk in. These are places worth remembering.

It is also important to note that all places on the planet are sacred because the earth is sacred. However, through the lens of

Spirit there are places where it feels like the veil is thin. It could be that these places received sacred worship for many years and that reverence is still palpable when you enter the space. There are places where great tragedies have happened and there is a sadness that you can feel when you walk on the land. All these things leave their spiritual and energetic mark, and we can feel that when we step into their locations.

For example, I was blessed to take a school trip to Washington, DC, when I was in middle school. We went to many sacred sites connected to the history of the United States. One of the places we visited was Gettysburg, Pennsylvania, at the site of a Civil War battle. I still have my notebook from that trip, and even my thirteen-year-old self noticed the heartache and pain at this location. I was overwhelmed by the thought of blood and death. I looked out over this field and all I could see was the bodies of young men. It was heart-wrenching and has stuck with me all these years later.

There was a great trauma that happened on the land in that location, and it is still upheld as the site of this trauma. The land has to tell this story over and over again on a daily basis. You can feel it. This history is a part of the land, and when we are open, we can hear that story being told.

The Veil Is Thin

In many religions, there is a belief in the separation between the physical world, where humans reside, and the spiritual world, which is the realm of the gods and/or spirits. Sadly, this belief has permeated many traditions, including Witchcraft and Paganism. The concept of a veil keeps the physical and the spiritual separate.

This separation of the mundane from the magical, or the physical from the spiritual, is sometimes referred to as "the veil." Think of what a veil is. It is a thin bit of fabric. It doesn't exactly stop you from seeing what is behind it, but it blurs it and makes it unclear. A veil can add an air of mystery and confusion to reality. A veil could be something beautiful and intriguing, much like works of Spirit.

Ultimately, a veil is a thing that separates.

Humans are not separate from what is holy or spiritual; we are holy and spiritual. It is this false separation that allows religions to create intermediaries that speak for the gods and set up a hierarchy in which only these intermediaries can access the spiritual realms and the rest of us have to go through them to access the spiritual.

The physical is not separate from the sacred; the physical is sacred. It is this separation that allows humans to cause so much damage to the earth and the environment.

There are many Witchcraft traditions that work with "the veil between the worlds" concept and take it one step further. The veil separates our physical world from other realms, realities, and magical places.[38] Those who practice with the veil also consider certain times of the year when the veil is thinner. During these times, it is easier for the spirit realm to communicate with us and it is easier for us to see what is happening on the other side.[39]

Is this true? In my experience, there are certain times of the year when it does feel easier to communicate with the otherworlds, but that's also because our overculture flows in the same way. Around Halloween, it feels spookier. It seems easier to connect with the dead then, but I communicate with the dead all year long.

In many traditions, such as Wicca, Samhain-tide, or the time around Halloween, is the time of year when the veil is thin and we can easily communicate with our beloved dead.[40] However, consider

38 Auryn, "The Veil Between the Worlds."
39 Beckett, "Thinking About the Veil Between the Worlds."
40 History.com editors, "Halloween 2025."

this: When it is Samhain-tide in the Northern Hemisphere, it is Beltane-tide in the Southern Hemisphere. So does this mean that the veil is thin only in the northern part of the planet at that time of year?

Many modern Witchcraft practices are based on traditions from Northern and Western Europe. These concepts and practices are beautiful, but they don't necessarily apply to other areas of the world. What happens where I live in Northern California is very different from what happens in Scotland, Wales, or Australia.

In my own personal practice, I've moved away from the thinking that the veil becomes thinner at specific times of the year. I tend to notice more when the veil feels thin in specific locations. It makes sense to me that we humans live in a reality adjacent to a myriad of "otherworlds." These realms could be where the gods live, where the fae reside, or where there are pockets of energy that can't be explained.

The sacred sites and locations that we might encounter are those where the veil is thin. They are places where we walk in and know that something is different. They have an otherworldly air about them. Whether they are famous and internationally known doesn't matter. What matters is that we recognize them when we enter one of them.

In my experience, there are places in the world where the spiritual feels closer to the surface. These places feel touched by Spirit. Is this due to the veil being thin or to spiritual residue hanging around? None of us can truly know, but ultimately I don't think it really matters.

Ley Lines

In 1925 an archaeologist by the name of Alfred Watkins wrote a book called *The Old Straight Track*, in which he coined the term *ley lines*. He posited that there are energetic lines that cross and crisscross the planet.[41] If you look at some of the more famous sacred sites in the world, they seem to line up and follow a pattern. Scientific proof of energetic lines following these lines has never been proven, but there is something to be said about the patterns and how these sacred sites seem to line up.

Ley lines are believed to carry spiritual energy and connect sacred sites all over the world. They create a weblike pattern across the globe. In places where ley lines cross, the spiritual energy is magnified. The points where these lines cross are considered power points.

I have been to some of these places where the lines cross and there is something that feels interesting there. Whether something is scientifically proven or not doesn't matter to me. You get to be the judge.

• • • •

The Foundation of Life and Magic

Dodie Graham McKay is a writer, Green Witch, and filmmaker inspired to document and share stories that capture the beauty of nature and the visible and invisible realms of magic and Witchcraft. She is the author of *Earth Magic* (Llewellyn, 2021) and *A Witch's Ally: Building a Magical Relationship with Familiars & Animal Companions* (Llewellyn, 2024). Her documentary films include *The WinniPagans*, *Starry Nights*, and the four-part series *Exploring the Sacred*. Dodie lives in Treaty One Territory, Winnipeg, Manitoba, Canada, where she spends her time walking her dogs and facilitating a busy coven.

41 Kershner, "What Are Ley Lines?"

AT THE BEGINNING of every human experience is earth. Without earth—as a planet, as an element, and sometimes even as a deity—we humans simply cannot exist. This celestial body, a swirling mass of rock, gas, and water, is an amazing and beautiful place where, by some remarkable chance, the elements of earth, air, fire, and water all found a place to become embodied and create life.

Element, Planet, or Deity?

As an element, earth represents the essential components for life: stability, sustenance, definition, boundaries, practicality, and fecundity. Earth moves slowly, deliberately; it is heavy and dense. It is loyal, responsible, ethical, and faithful. Earth may not be as dynamic, free-spirited, or exciting as other elements, but it is steadfast and dependable—a solid and trustworthy ally for both magic and mundane life.

Earth is also a place—a planet, our home. It is the physical manifestation of the attributes associated with the element of earth. We humans are rooted here, entirely dependent on Earth's life-giving ability—the food, shelter, plants, animals, and resources it provides for us so generously and unwaveringly. Our planet evolved slowly, over hundreds of millions of years, to reach the point where humans could develop, and it will likely remain here for millennia after we are gone.

In order to understand our place on Earth, human beings have, since the beginning of our history, sought to commune with the life force that brought about creation. Our inherent curiosity and sense of wonder compel us to understand our environment and seek answers from beings greater than ourselves. We crave assurance from a higher power that life has meaning and that there may be order and balance available to comfort and motivate us. This pattern has been repeated throughout history and across cultures. Humans have turned to the obvious giver of structure and abundance, Mother Earth in her many names, forms, and faces, to worship, give thanks, and ask for help. We have recognized Earth as sacred and as a life-giving parental figure. This reverence is extended into the land, sea, and sky.

Spirits of Earth

Alongside Mother Earth is a retinue of earth spirits that occupy and animate the landscape. These are the beings we sense when we are out in nature, watching us as we explore the wild places and open ourselves to the presence of the life force in the natural world. Devas, dryads, nymphs, gnomes, fairies, dwarves, little people, wee folk, genius loci, spirits of place, and many more can all be potential allies and helpers to humans—if we can be patient, receptive, and considerate enough to endear ourselves to them.

Earth in Practice

Whenever we set our minds to do sacred or magical work or commune with any type of spirit, the first thing we do is connect to Earth. We ground ourselves, rooting our consciousness in the earth beneath our feet, in order to stabilize and orient ourselves. Perhaps we gather tools made from natural materials of the earth—wood, metal, antler, or stone. These items are stimuli, physical artifacts that evoke a sense of mystery, wonder, and connection to magic and spirit. We select a place to do our work, indoors or outdoors. These places are usually where we feel safe and secluded, more able to connect with spirit. We create these sacred spaces out of a desire to establish a special earthly point of contact with otherworldly things. We may choose to erect an altar or designate a particular compass point, plant, rock, or landform as our focal point—a spot on Earth where the presence of spirit feels more imminent or intense.

Water, air, and fire, when they are literal, are also part of the earthly realm. The element of fire comes to us as a flame—burning and destroying, but also cleansing and clearing the way for new things to develop. We need its heat, and we are drawn to its movement and spontaneity—forever moving, changing, and transforming. Water flows to us in trickles and torrents, in great oceans and muddy puddles. The ebb and flow of how we see it reflects our own emotions, dreams, and intuition—rising and falling like a tide. Our bodies make salty tears—of joy and sorrow, feelings of ecstasy and despair—from the depths of who we are. Air arrives as our ideas, inspirations, and thoughts—the processes within our minds. With our breath, we speak them and bring them into being. They are carried on the wind, through the atmosphere, and into the world.

There is no separating the human experience from earth. We are made of it. Our bodies are a composite of the elements, made whole, bound together, and embodied by the physical properties of earth. It is earth that gives body to the passion and movement of fire, tempered with the feeling and emotion of water and the intelligence and imagination of air. It is in this embodied form that humans have developed the methods to reach beyond the physical and satisfy our longing to be something greater, more enlightened, and to touch the realm of Spirit.

Dodie Graham McKay

• • • •

Vortices

Vortexes, or vortices, are locations where spiritual energy is concentrated. These areas often hold more spiritual energy than other places and spiritual seekers tend to be drawn to them.

A vortex, scientifically speaking, is when there is a rotation of energy around an axis. Vortices in nature can be seen in water whirlpools, dust devils, and smoke rings. The energy of a vortex moves both upward and downward. Spiritual vortices are the same except they are made of spiritual energy, which is much harder to track and to prove.

There are famous vortex sites all over the world, but there are also vortices that aren't as well-known. You could easily have one in your own backyard! Some believe you can also create a spiritual vortex of energy with the right configuration of crystals, stones, and energy movement. And there are vortices that come and go, perhaps never even noticed by humans.

Here are some famous vortex sites:

- Sedona, Arizona, United States
- La Senda, Costa Rica
- Nauyaca, Costa Rica
- Table Mountain, South Africa
- Haleakala volcano, Hawaii, United States
- Es Vedra, Ibiza, Spain
- Lake Rotopounamu, New Zealand
- Uluru, Australia
- Lake Titicaca, Peru
- Kuh-i-Malik Salih, Afghanistan

CHAPTER 4

Sacred Spirit Sites

There are specific sacred Spirit sites all over the world that are famous or infamous. People travel thousands of miles to visit these places, often as a devotional act or pilgrimage. Each one of these sacred places has its own unique energy signature. Not all are created equal.

Abu Simbel

Abu Simbel is a temple located in southern Egypt. Outside the temple are two sixty-six-foot-tall sculptures of Ramses II. The temple was dedicated to the sun gods and is a marvel of building and design. Two times a year, the sun shines through the doors and on the inner temple, illuminating the inner shrine. Its alignment with the sun, as a sun temple, is what makes this temple a marvel of Spirit.[42]

Big Horn Medicine Wheel

This Indigenous sacred site is located in the Big Horn Mountains of Wyoming in the United States. The Medicine Wheel is a prehistoric site and an important location for the Indigenous tribes that originated in the Wyoming area. Although there are medicine wheels located all over the continent, this is the first one to be studied. It is likely a calendar, as it lines up with celestial bodies.[43]

Crater Lake

Crater Lake is located in Oregon in the United States. It is the deepest lake in the country and is the seventh deepest in the world. It sits in the caldera of a volcano and isn't connected to any other

42 Encyclopædia Britannica editors, "Abu Simbel."

43 Chapman, "Medicine Wheel/Medicine Mountain: Celebrated and Controversial Landmark."

bodies of water. The crater came from an ancient volcanic eruption and is filled with water due to annual snowfall.[44]

Golden Temple

The Golden Temple is located in Amritsar, Punjab, India. It is a temple for Sikhs, but beyond that tradition it is a place of community and equality. The shrine has four entrances, symbolizing that anyone from any place is welcome.[45]

Mecca

The site of Mecca, or Makkah in Arabic, is the most sacred place in the world for those of the Muslim faith. This location is believed to be the birthplace of the Prophet Mohammed. It is a requirement of every member of the Islamic faith to make a pilgrimage to Mecca at least once in their lives. Mecca is located in Saudi Arabia and hosts millions of visitors each year.

Mount Shasta

Mount Shasta is part of a volcanic mountain range located in Northern California in the United States. It has been the site of spiritual activity and mystery since before colonization. The tribes native to the area believed it was the home of many spirits and deities. There have been a lot of weird recorded events over the years, like the openings of caves moving or disappearing altogether. Some believe the mythological people from Atlantis or Lemuria live inside the mountain.[46]

44 Oregon Explorer, "Facts About Crater Lake."
45 GoldenTempleAmritsar.org, "The Golden Temple Amritsar."
46 Alpenglow Expeditions, "A Brief History of Mt. Shasta."

Sistine Chapel

The Sistine Chapel is located within the Vatican. It is the location of the papal conclave, where new popes are selected. It is decorated by frescoes covering the ceiling that Michaelangelo painted in the early 1500s. The frescoes are of the stories of Genesis from the Bible. When visitors arrive at this sacred site, they are asked to keep silent as a sign of reverence and respect.[47]

Stonehenge

This Neolithic site is located in England. It is a large circle of stones that seem to be placed to line up with the sun on the summer and winter solstices, but the truth is we don't know what the original builders of this magnificent site used it for. Stonehenge's use has melted into legend, but history buffs and magical practitioners from all over the world still visit this location.[48]

Uluru

This Indigenous sacred site is located in the southern part of the Northern Territories in Australia. It is a large sandstone monolith that stands alone in the middle of the landscape. Uluru is a sacred site for the Anangu people, the Aboriginal people of the area, and is honored as the home of the primordial Earth Mother. There are petroglyphs and ancient art across the sandstone.[49]

Varanasi

The city of Varanasi is located on the Ganges River in India and is considered one of the most important sacred sites of the Hindu faith. According to myth and tradition, anyone who dies in this location will be freed from the cycle of reincarnation, able to move

47 Musei Vaticani, "Sistine Chapel."
48 English Heritage, "History of Stonehenge."
49 Uluru Australia, "What Is Uluru?"

into the next state of being. Millions visit this city every year and wash in the waters of the sacred Ganges River.[50]

The Wailing Wall

The Wailing Wall, also called the Western Wall, is a sacred site in Jerusalem. It has been a sacred site for the Jewish people going back to 587 BCE. It is tradition to push small pieces of paper with prayers or blessings written on them into the cracks in the wall. It is a pilgrimage site for many of the Jewish faith.[51]

Sacred Sites Near You

You don't have to travel to the other side of the world to find sacred sites. The best way to honor sacred Spirit locations is to find the ones near to you and give them some of your love and respect. You can start this by researching. Look up your location and see if there are already places that are considered "sacred." Where is there a history of worship or reverence?

If you live on colonized land, like I do, it might take more digging to discover the places that were considered sacred. It is also important to check in with local tribal practices to make sure that visiting one of these sacred sites would not interfere with any current Indigenous practices that may be happening in that location.

If you do the research and don't come up with a lot, look to national, regional, and local parks. These places of nature often hold an energy of reverence because they have been selected to be held as untouched by development. Many of these places already appeal to more spiritually inclined people. These spots have likely already had magic done on or around them.

50 Varanasi, "History."

51 Encyclopædia Britannica editors, "Western Wall."

The next step is to visit these places. Go for a hike or a walk. Notice if you can feel a vibe or an energy that suggests something is different about this location.

For example, there is a regional park very close to where I live. The park is beautiful and there are lots of walking trails and places to explore across the acres of land marked out as part of the park. However, there is one grove of oak trees that feels particularly sacred. It is lovely to look at and being in this place feels magical. The park has benches and barbecues set up for gatherings and events, but these things only seem to add to the energy of sacredness and not take away from it.

This place has an energy that is different from the rest of the park. When you step into the grove of trees, you feel like you are entering a different realm. It feels magical and unique. This is one of my local sacred sites. It won't be on any website or map. No one has written about it, and no international visitors are seeking it out, but this location is sacred to me.

No doubt you can already think of places you love that feel sacred to you. It doesn't have to be a wild or natural place. It could be a human-created structure or building. It could be anywhere that feels special to you. These sacred Spirit sites are all over the world.

Honoring Local Spirits of Place

When you find a local Spirit site that you want to work with, there are some great ways to engage with the energies of this place. What is important is to listen to the land and make sure that what you are doing feels in alignment with the desires of the space.

It is also important to never leave anything behind that could cause damage. Don't leave offerings that aren't biodegradable out in the natural world. It is also important to do a little research on what could be harmful to the land. Don't leave seeds that could sprout invasive plants. Don't leave water as an offering unless you know it won't damage the plants. Even an offering left with a clear and open heart can be harmful. With a little research, you can make sure anything you leave behind in a natural space won't cause harm.

One of the easiest things you can do to help a local sacred site is to pick up garbage. This might not feel exceptionally witchy or glamorous, but there are rarely places in the world without litter. Keeping a sacred site free of detritus is an excellent way to show you care about the place. I like to keep a bag and some gloves in my car at all times just in case I find myself in a place that really needs some help. Again, it's not the most glamorous side of Witchcraft, but it is very important to the health of a wild place.

Spending time at a sacred site is another good way to connect with the energy of it. Go for walks, have picnics, meditate while sitting in the space, hold simple ceremonies, and do these things as a way to feel the energy of the place and introduce your energy to it.

Building small shrines is another way to engage with a place's energy. However, be cautious with this type of ritual. Only use biodegradable objects and nothing that could harm the natural environment. If you want to create a mandala or some other form of beauty using items from the natural landscape, be sure it doesn't damage the natural flora and fauna of the place.

For example, scooping up big piles of leaves can cause problems for insect populations. Stacking stones in a creek can lead to injuring some of the wildlife if the stones should fall over. These things might look beautiful and they may have been created from a place of the heart, but ultimately they aren't healthy for the site. It is important to be very mindful and humble while engaging with the arms of the wild places.

Of course, money always works to help sacred sites, especially if they are places where the public is likely to visit. Donating money to local causes that help with upkeep, buying local, and putting your money where your mouth is are all ways to help local sacred sites.

EXERCISE: Connecting with Spirits of the Land

This exercise comes from my book *What Is Remembered Lives*. I included a section about working with the fae, but in my experience the spirits of the land and the fae either are closely related and/or are the same thing.

This exercise requires a sit spot. This is a place out in the wild or a natural area where you can simply sit and watch. It is common for hunters and trackers to have sit spots in order to notice the signs of animals.

When looking for a sit spot, consider the following:

- Running water: Sites with running water will bring various types of spirits. Locations where there is a lot of animal activity will often cross over with spirit activity.
- Liminal space: Liminal spaces call to Spirit because they are neither one thing nor another but both—for example, a beach. Beaches are not the sea nor the land. Spirits are drawn to these places.

Needs

It's time to set up your sit spot and get comfortable. You want to blend in with the landscape and become a part of it. You will need:

Something to sit on

Water

Journal and pen

Directions

Sit, calm your breathing, and pay attention to your surroundings. Watch the plants and animals. What are they doing? Watch what is happening out of the corner of your eyes. What is happening in your periphery? Pay attention to the shimmers and the shadows. Allow yourself to become a part of the land.

Drink your water as you need it. Write down things as you notice them. When you feel complete, thank the land for spending time with you and clean up your spot.

Personal Sacred Spirit Sites

For all the big or ancient sites that exist in the world, there are thousands of small Spirit sites that are special to only one family or a single individual. These places are unlikely to make it into any travel guides, but their power to the family or individual is just as important as that of a place that is visited by millions of tourists every year.

Cemeteries

Typically, cemeteries are sacred only to the people who visit them. People leave offerings for those they know who have died and are interred there. When you visit a cemetery where there is a loved one resting there, you feel a connection to that place. It becomes a part of your relationship with the one who has crossed over. However, cemeteries can also be places to seek out Spirit, even if you don't know anyone buried there.

Ancestor Shrines

Ancestral shrines are common in most East Asian cultures, but their popularity in Western traditions, Witchcraft, Wicca, and folk traditions has grown over the last few decades. Ancestor shrines are altars for your ancestors in your living space. These shrines can be for your beloved dead, those who have passed over in your lifetime, or for your ancestors, those you never met in life. An ancestor shrine can be as simple as a picture of your beloved dead, a candle, and a glass of water.

Home Altars

Home altars serve a wide range of purposes. You might have a home altar for the seasons, for a deity, for a spell, or to connect with ancestors. Home altars are your personal connection to Spirit in whatever form you feel called. Home altars are highly personal because they are created by you. Whatever the altar is for, it takes your creative input to make it happen.

Ritual Locations

Any place where a ritual has taken place has the potential to be a sacred Spirit site. For example, my local Witchcraft community has held a Beltane ritual at a local location for decades. The site of this ritual is considered sacred to our local community. It holds a piece of our community's Spirit from all the rituals that have taken place there.

Conclusion

Sacred Spirit sites could be literally anywhere. You could be sitting in one right now! From world-known locations to the small and nearby, a sacred site holds the energy of Spirit. The more you visit them and seek them out, the more their energy and connection to Spirit grows.

PART 2

WORKING WITH THE ELEMENT OF SPIRIT

"Enjoyment is an incredible energizer to the human spirit."

—John C. Maxwell

Chapter 5

THE ELEMENT OF SPIRIT IN MAGIC

The way Spirit folds into your magical practice is really up to you. You determine what you want your relationship with Spirit to be like. There are some traditional ways that Spirit shows up in our collective and lineage magical practices. As with all magical practice, the way to work with Spirit is highly personal. Trust your instincts and listen to your intuition.

Discernment

The Witch's most powerful tool is discernment. Forget all the athames, wands, and pentacles; discernment is where it's at. Discernment is a tool of Spirit because it is something that can't be explained. You've either got it or you don't. The good news is that you can develop your discernment. You can make it stronger, just like a muscle. The more you use it, the better it gets.

The meaning of the word discernment is the ability to judge well. This sounds easy. We all have an inner judge, but having strong discernment isn't about being judgmental. Being judgmental doesn't come from a place of high power, but having strong discernment does. To know if something is a scam or a lie or if someone is untrustworthy, you need to have a good sense of discernment. I will say, in this modern age of social media and filters, it's hard to know what to trust. Social media can make it feel like we can't even trust our eyes! And that's why you need to work on your discernment.

The more your discernment is active, the easier it is to hear your intuition. These two things are closely related. That gut reaction you get when first meeting someone is your intuition. How you utilize that information is your discernment.

Casting the Circle

Many Witches and Pagans perform their magic in a ritual circle. When we make an energetic circle around our ritual space, we are creating a barrier. This energetic barrier helps to hold the energy of the working in and keep any unwanted influences out. The process of "casting the circle," as it is often called, is connected to the energy of Spirit.

Creating a demarcation that what happens inside of this space is sacred and therefore outside of time and space is exactly what the element of Spirit is all about.

There are dozens of ways to cast a circle. Some traditions follow very specific rules. One form is not better than another. They are all just different steps in a similar dance. You might create an energetic barrier, a literal circle with salt, rope, or chalk, or you might speak specific words toward the corners of the space. There are plenty of ways to separate the ritual circle from the mundane world.

Tools of Spirit

The tools of the element of Spirit can be used for a wide variety of purposes. Since Spirit is ephemeral, you might not even connect a specific ritual tool to Spirit. Because Spirit is the all and the nothing the same can be said of the tools that are connected to this element. However, if you want tangible physical tools for Spirit, the following are great options.

Altars and Shrines

Altars of any type are connected to the element of Spirit. Any place where you are performing your magic, connecting with spirits, or connecting with your own spiritual being is a place of Spirit. Altars come in many shapes and forms. There isn't one "right" way to build or create an altar. A lot of altar creation is about what appeals to your spiritual self. Here are just a few examples of the types of altars you might build.

Working Altar

Working altars may be temporary or permanent, but they are the location of spellwork. You may set up a working altar for a spell and then clean it up when the spell is complete, or you may have a working altar for an ongoing spell that stays up all the time.

Shrine for a Deity

A shrine for a deity is a place of reverence for that entity. An altar for a specific god should have imagery of the spirit. There should be a way to make offerings, and it should appeal to the god that it is created for.

Shrine for Ancestors

A shrine for ancestors is a place of reverence for your ancestors. These can be ancestors of blood or spirit. As with an altar for a deity, you should be able to make offerings and have images of your beloved dead, and it should represent your ancestors.

Seasonal Altar

A seasonal altar is set up just for the season. It is a representation of the cycle of the Wheel of the Year. With a seasonal altar, it is appropriate to change the colors and decor to match the season.

Traveling Altar

A traveling altar is one that is small enough to take with you. It can be for a specific spell, a shrine, or anything else you can dream up. The key is to keep it very small so it can easily go anywhere with you.

Hidden Altar

Any of the above can be a hidden altar. The difference is that you might not know by looking at it that it is an altar. This is best when living with people who may not be open to having altars. One example of a hidden altar is creating an ancestor altar using family photos all in one spot with one simple candle. This is an ancestor shrine, but no one would know it.

Cauldrons

In my early days of practicing Witchcraft, I was taught that the main tool of the element of Spirit was the cauldron. The cauldron is a place of transformation. What goes into a cauldron comes out changed. Cauldrons and cooking pots have long magical histories in cultures across the globe. In many of these myths and stories, the cauldron is a place of transformation. It is a container of magic. It's no wonder that, even with cooking pots and cauldrons being used for household needs rather than magical purposes, the cauldron still holds a fascination for people.

Containers

Containers with any spiritual use are connected to Spirit. Just as the element of Spirit is connected to the process of casting the circle, which is an energetic or spiritual container, any physical containers used in ritual are in the realm of Spirit. Here are some containers you might find:

- Mirror boxes
- Tarot boxes or wraps
- Jar and bottle spells
- Cauldrons
- Bowls where ingredients are mixed

Mind-Altering Substances

In some traditions, the use of mind-altering substances is a common practice. This is not to say that you must (or need to) use mind-altering substances, and in many places they are illegal. However, psychedelics and the like are known to open up the mind and allow people to see and experience the world around them from an unfiltered place. There are other ways to get into a mind-altered space without the use of substances. Breathwork, meditation, deprivation, and other activities can bring on similar states of awareness. Being able to shift the mind or shift awareness is the realm of Spirit and the magic of this element. If you decide to use mind-altering substances, do so only with the proper care and supervision.

Statuary or Deity Symbols

Statues and other forms of representation for deities are connected to Spirit. People often work with a deity sculpture that has been "ensouled," meaning the energy of the deity has been invoked into the statuary. There is an actual spirit in that statue. When this happens, it is important to take care of that statue. It is now literally a part of the god it represents. However, whether a statue is ensouled or not, any deity representation is a way to have Spirit in your altar space.

CHAPTER 5

Language

Language, speech, and communication keep us grounded in the tangible world. However, there are ways to use language as a means of connecting with Spirit. By using a language other than the one we are comfortable using, our first language, we can bypass our thinking mind and get more into the flow of Spirit.

Theban Script

The Theban alphabet is often referred to as the Witch's alphabet. It has origins in the early 1500s, when Johannes Trithemius used it in his book *Polygraphia*, in which he said the alphabet was created by Honorius of Thebes. This system of writing became popular in the early occult movement of the 1900s. Some Wiccans only use this alphabet when writing in their book of shadows to keep their writing secret. Theban script is connected to Spirit because it is a way to keep your writing hidden in plain sight. It has been used as a magical alphabet for hundreds of years, and the more people use it in their magical work, the more magical the script becomes.

Hebrew

Hebrew is known as the holy tongue and is the language of the Jewish people and the country of Israel. This language and the letters are often used in occult writings and practices. In the Bible, this language is referred to as Lashon Hakodesh. The writings of the Old Testament were written in Hebrew, which makes it a spiritual language with ancient origins. Judaism has a long history of being connected to the occult and can be found in many historical grimoires. Its use in ceremonial and other forms of magic makes it a good language for Spirit magic.

Any Foreign Language

When you speak a language in ritual that is not your native tongue, it can help open you up to Spirit. This is especially true if you speak the ancient language of a deity that is not your first language. It can be a challenge to speak in a language you don't actually know, but it is a powerful way to bypass your logical self and connect directly with Spirit.

Glossolalia

Glossolalia, also known as speaking in tongues, is a practice many religions use to direct communication with the Spirit. When people speak in tongues, they are allowing the Spirit to move through them. The language often sounds like gibberish to those listening, but occasionally prophecy or oracles can be heard through the speaker.

• • • •

Breath and Sea

Astrea Taylor is an eclectic pagan Witch, the author of *Air Magic, Intuitive Witchcraft*, and *Inspiring Creativity Through Magick*, and the coauthor of *Modern Witchcraft with the Greek Gods*. She has written passages for several periodicals and books, including *Mastering Magick*, *Llewellyn's Spell-A-Day Almanac*, *Llewellyn's Magical Almanac*, and *We'Moon*. Her life goals include empowering other magical practitioners and encouraging them to use intuition in their Craft. In her books and classes, she shares her love of science, magic, history, mental health, and energy awareness. Learn more at AstreaTaylor.com.

Embodying the element of air in your spirit elevates your perspective to be more empowered. It fuels your imagination, inspiration, and ability to envision. There's so much magic to be found hidden in the air around you, and spirit magic lets you access it.

Following is a meditation that will help you awaken, align, and use the strengths of the two elements to enhance your magical abilities. If you wish, light incense or inhale some essential oils during the practice, or simply imagine that you can smell the inspiring aromas.

Begin Your Meditation

To begin, inhale deeply. Send the fresh air directly to the center of your body. Allow the refreshing qualities of air to awaken and nourish your spirit. You may notice a stirring sensation within. Take another deep inhalation of the living air and let your spirit fully awaken.

As you continue to breathe into your spirit, you may feel a rush of energy or a sensation of expansion. With each breath, give your spirit the freedom to become larger than your body and take up more of the space in the air around it. If your spirit feels elevated, breathe into that sensation.

Imagine that you're inhaling energy from the vast, invisible ocean of air that surrounds you. Let your breaths be like waves. On your exhalations, wash away any old ideas or mental constructs that keep you from experiencing the true majesty of your spirit. Release the mental burdens of the past and anything that you don't wish to retain. With your inhalations, allow a cleansing energy to wash over you, renewing your spirit. Continue until your spirit feels fully awakened and cleansed.

On the next inhalation, set an intention to align your spirit with the element of air. You may feel a slight shift in your aura (the energetic field in the air around you). You may also experience an activation sensation in your lungs, throat, mouth, third eye, or the top of your head. If so, let them be fed and recharged by your breath.

Begin to breathe with a frequency of inhalations and exhalations to actively engage your mind and spirit at the same time. Your breath rate should be a pace that you can sustain for a few minutes. Ideally it should help you find the magic of the present moment and the presence of your best self.

Magical Possibilities

You have many options at this point in the work. You can stay in this field of energy and simply experience the bliss of mind-spirit connection or you can do some air-spirit magic to enhance your life. Here are some other possibilities:

- If you have grappled with a situation, you can call upon the powers of objectivity and discernment to know the truth. You can set boundaries and sever cords that are not beneficial. You can cleanse your aura or the air in your home. You may choose to set magical intentions with this mindset, then speak the words to activate them. You could strengthen your mental pathways so your thought patterns naturally support your magical intentions. You could even call upon the spirits of air or imagine a living temple in the sky to act as a beacon to your desires.
- Envision the outcome you desire, knowing the powers of spirit and air support you.

Coming Down

When you want to come down from the union of elements, modify your breath to a rhythm that helps you ground into your body. You may want to look at your feet, shake off the excess energy, or give yourself a hug. This beneficial practice can be used regularly or whenever you need perspective. Trust your breath to lead your spirit. The more you engage these two elements together, the easier it becomes, as those mental roads are reinforced every time you travel them.

Astrea Taylor

• • • •

Symbols of Spirit

The traditional symbol attached to Spirit is the pentacle, the five-pointed star with a circle around it. This symbol represents all five elements working together in unison: Earth, Air, Fire, Water, and Spirit. Each element is connected to one of the points of the star, and the circle around them is what brings them all together.

Colors of Spirit

The colors most often associated with Spirit are black, white, and gray. However, any color that is connected to a liminality will fit the bill. The colors of a sunrise or sunset, for example, would also belong to Spirit.

Astrology

Astrology is the study of the stars and planets and how the symbolism of their movements is reflected in our lives. Alchemists used astrology to try to understand the Aether, or Spirit.

Each planet, star, and celestial body moves according to its own unique cycle. There is a whole dance happening in the heavens all the time. The practice of tracking the stars and interpreting their patterns is something that has been going on for millennia. There is evidence that the ancient Babylonians were tracking the stars in the twelfth century BCE, and the twelve-house system used in modern astrology is based on their system. This system migrated to India and then to Greece, with each culture leaving its mark on the system we use today.

The ancient Greeks named the planets for their gods. Then the Romans adopted the same system but used their own names for the gods, which we still use today. This same astrological system has had a major impact on Arabic and European cultures as well.

Other astrological systems have their own rhythms and calendars unrelated to the modern astrology that most of us are familiar with. The ancient Mayan calendar is one of them. The Mayans split the turning of time into different systems from what we use for our modern calendar, and the same is true of the Hindu system and several other East Asian calendars. They each have their own way of tracking the stars, but the modern astrological system that is prevalent today has its roots in ancient Babylon.

All twelve zodiac signs are connected to the traditional elements of Earth, Air, Fire, and Water. Three zodiac signs fall under the influence of each of these elements. But Spirit also exists in the symbols and nuances of astrology. When it comes to astrology and Spirit, the following are some of the more important aspects to consider.

Birth Charts

Astrology is much more than just reading your sun sign forecast in a fashion magazine every month. At the core of astrology is the birth chart. The idea is that when each of us is born, the sky and the constellations are doing a specific thing. A birth chart is a snapshot of the sky at the moment you were born. It is believed that your birth chart can reveal things that you can expect out of life. It can reveal how a person's personality might develop, what their strengths and weaknesses are, and how to best utilize their skills.

In modern astrology, the sky is split into twelve houses, and each house is connected to a specific sign. Your personal individual layout and how the houses show up in your chart will be unique. Add on top of that all the planets and where they are in the sky and you get quite a complicated map. Astrology is so much more than your sun sign.

Knowing your birth chart is a way to know your spirit. A birth chart can reveal things, explain things, and at the very least give you a heavenly body to blame for some of your bad habits. I say that last part in jest, but knowing the basics of your chart can be very powerful.

There are plenty of websites and apps that will calculate your birth chart for free. I'm a fan of the Chani astrology app. It's filled with personal and collective astrology information, and there are weekly podcasts about what the stars are up to that week.

If you want to dig deep into the nuances of your birth chart, seek out a professional astrologer who can help you translate what is going on in your chart into actions and ideas. An astrologer knows how to analyze what is going on in the stars in terms of your specific chart and can give you ideas about challenges or successes that might be headed your way.

Ninth House

The Ninth House is the house of spirituality and greater wisdom. This house sits at the top of the chart, which is sometimes described as an opening into the world from the heavens. The Ninth House is ruled by the sign of Sagittarius, but your birth chart will reveal what sign is connected to this house in your chart, based on your time of birth. No matter what that particular sign is, the energy of the Ninth House is influenced by Sagittarius, which is wisdom-seeking and spiritual.

Twelfth House

The Twelfth House is the house of hidden meanings, the imagination, and the subconscious. Unseen shadows or sorrow can reveal themselves in this house. The Twelfth House is ruled by Pisces, but your birth chart will reveal what sign is connected to this house in your own chart, based on your time of birth. No matter what that particular sign is, the energy of the Twelfth House house is influenced by Pisces, which is intuitive and dreamy.

Jupiter

In astrology, Jupiter is the planet of luck, abundance, and growth. How this planet shows up in your birth chart can reveal the best ways to expand your horizons. Jupiter is a planet that has a lot of good energy and can help you seek out adventures and success.

Lot of Spirit

The idea of a Lot of Spirit comes from the Hermetic system of astrology. It is a mathematical calculation that tells where your spiritual house is based on your birth chart. The Lot of Spirit will explain what the character of your soul is. Understanding this astrological placement can also help you get in touch with your spirit guides. Most online astrology systems don't include the Lot of Spirit; it is a deeper dive into your chart.[52]

Tarot

Tarot cards belong in the realm of Spirit because they are a way to connect with the messages of your intuition. The tarot started out as a simple deck of playing cards used for games. These playing cards had a series of "trump" cards that were often radical or provocative for the time. These cards popped up in several European countries around the same time, so it is impossible to determine where the tarot originated. But its popularity grew and several countries, including France, Spain, and Italy, all claim to be the home of tarot cards. The oldest tarot deck we have a record of is the Visconti-Sforza, which was created for the Duchy of Milan in the 1500s. Over time, the tarot, which started as a card game, became a vehicle for fortune-telling.

Modern tarot decks are most often based on a system created by Arthur Waite and Pamela Colman Smith. Arthur Waite was a member of the Golden Dawn spiritual community and created a tarot deck with the rites, tools, and beliefs of the Golden Dawn interwoven into the cards' symbolism. Pamela Colman Smith took his concepts and created the imagery in the Rider-Waite-Smith deck. This deck contains seventy-eight cards, with four suits and twenty-two trump cards. It was first published in 1909. Since that time, many others have created their own decks, using their own artwork and sometimes different meanings for the cards. Now there are thousands of tarot decks based on the 1909 version.

52 Wen, "Hermetic Lots (Arabic Parts)."

Major Arcana

The tarot can be split into two sets of cards. There is the minor arcana, which is made up of the four suits mentioned above. These suits correlate to the elements. The suit of Pentacles connects to Earth, the suit of Cups to Water, the suit of Wands to Fire, and the suit of Swords to Air. These cards are practically the same as a regular deck of playing cards, with each suit having cards ace through ten and four face cards, Page, Knight, Queen, and King.

The major arcana are true cards of Spirit in the tarot. These cards can be seen as the path of initiation. Each of the cards has a deep spiritual meaning:

0 The Fool: the beginning of the journey
1 The Magician: gathering the tools and skills needed
2 The High Priestess: tuning into the inner wisdom
3 The Empress: achievement, fertility, and abundance; big mom energy
4 The Emperor: leadership, structure, and boundaries; big dad energy
5 The Hierophant: religion, learning, and dedication to the spiritual path
6 The Lovers: finding that deep connection, union, and surrender
7 The Chariot: moving forward in the journey, success, and winning
8 Strength: stepping into power, having confidence and faith
9 The Hermit: turning within for counsel, meditation, and inner guidance
10 The Wheel of Fortune: the cycle turning, synchronicity, and gain
11 Justice: using judgment, being fair, and finding balance

12 The Hanged Man: seeking wisdom through the action of surrender
13 Death: the ending of something, initiation, and change
14 Temperance: finding balance, alchemy, and stepping into truth
15 The Devil: checking on unhealthy obsessions, doing things outside the norm
16 The Tower: intense and dramatic change, destruction and things collapsing
17 The Star: finding deep healing, dipping into intuition and hope
18 The Moon: uncovering secrets, seeing what has been hidden, hidden fears
19 The Sun: stepping into profound joy, success, freedom, and happiness
20 Judgement: hearing the call to step into something bigger, transformation
21 The World: the end of the journey, success and completion

The major arcana can provide spiritual guidance when you're going through a challenging time or rite of passage. Following this path is the walking of the path of Spirit.

The Four Virtues

Four of the major arcana cards are referred to as the four virtues. Virtues are considered positive character traits that are often tied together with the keys to being a good religious person. In Islam, Hinduism, and Christianity, there are different virtues to pursue to be a good practitioner of that faith. In the tarot system, the four virtues are fortitude, temperance, justice, and prudence. Plato wrote about the four virtues in book 4 of *The Republic*. These concepts were his system of ethics. These ethical concepts are "hidden" in the tarot system. Temperance is the Temperance card—clearly. Fortitude is the Strength card. Justice, again obviously, is the Justice card. Prudence is hotly debated. Some say this card has fallen out of usage, but others connect this card to the Hermit.

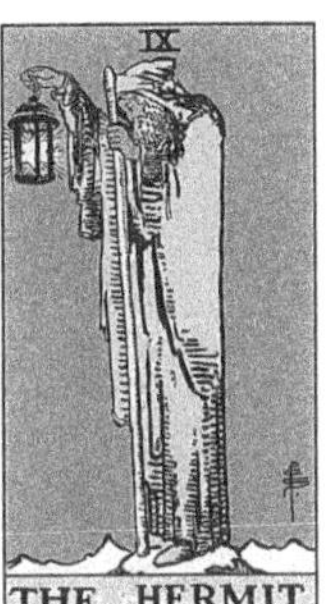

Drawing Down

Drawing down the moon is a term that comes from the Wiccan traditions. It is the practice of assumption or possession by a deity. Other Witchcraft and magical systems might refer to this process as aspecting, drawing down, trance possession, or being ridden. Some use the term *drawing down the moon* to refer to calling in female deities only and *drawing down the sun* to refer to calling in male deities only.

Different traditions have different rules about this process of sharing your body with a deity. The way that I was taught is that there are different levels of aspecting.

Influence

When you call upon a god in a ritual by invocation or evocation, you are inviting the *influence* of that god into the flow of the ritual. You might feel their influence upon you, as if you are wearing them as a cloak, or as a presence in the room. Their energy can be felt, but it is an external experience, not an internal one.

Aspecting

The middle step between influence and possession is called *aspecting*. With this technique, you invite deities to share your body but not fully take it over. With an aspecting experience, you often have a relationship with the deity ahead of time. And before stepping into the process, there are agreements made between you and the deity that you are about to invoke. With this type of process, the person aspecting will often have some memory of the experience.

Possession

Full *possession* is when a deity completely takes over your body. This is a process that takes some time. Typically, rituals with full trance possessions are daylong rituals where there is a lot of drumming, chanting, and singing to call to the specific spirits. The person who is "ridden" by the god will usually have no recollection of what took place.

Aspecting and possession are advanced techniques that should not be taken on without training and practice. However, influence is a good way to start the process of drawing down. I will delve more deeply into this topic in chapter 10.

Intentions of Spirit in Magic

Every element has specific magical energetics that it is better at connecting with. Some spells will be more effective when focused with a specific element. When working spells that have a Spirit energetic, you will find that many of them are about personal and spiritual growth—no real surprise there. The following spells are best to work with a focus or intention of Spirit:

- Self-growth: spells for improving one's character, growing in skills, or switching from a negative habit to a positive one
- The Sight: spells for increasing psychic abilities, sharpening intuition, or opening to communication with spirits
- Spiritual awareness: spells for stronger discernment, tuning into the subtle parts of nature, or connecting with the unseen
- The Divine: spells to work with deities and other entities

Theurgy

Theurgy is a word that comes to us from the Neoplatonists. It is the practice of inviting spirits into a ritual space in order to gain their influence and/or power. Many of the rituals used to raise these spirits can be found in the book *The Key of Solomon*, which is an ancient book of spells and rituals. These rituals include drawing symbols on the ground, speaking incantations, and using ritual tools. This type of ritual is often referred to as high magic.

Akashic Records

The Akashic records are the etheric spiritual catalog of all that has ever happened as well as all that *will* ever happen. These "records" exist on the astral plane and can be accessed by anyone, assuming you know how to reach them and read them. The Akashic records have been described as the universe's supercomputer.

Practitioners who work with the Akashic records will train in how to access and read them to help others learn what they need for their important life lessons. However, anyone with the desire can locate these records and utilize them for spiritual growth.

Edgar Cayce was one of the Spiritualists who made the Akashic records more well-known. He was a Spiritualist in the late 1800s and early 1900s. Cayce has been referred to as the "sleeping prophet" because he would go into a trance state and give people readings on their lives, loves, and health using the Akashic records as his way of gaining information.[53]

When Cayce was asked how he was able to perform these readings, he responded that there were two keys to his success: One was to connect to the subconscious of his client and the second was to read the Akashic records.

The Akashic records can also be thought of as the superconsciousness of humanity. We are all connected to this consciousness; every human is one of the threads woven into the tapestry. By accessing our own thread, we can then gain access to the larger group of "records."

When I access the Akashic records, I see them as a huge, beautifully bound book. When I go into the records to seek information, I ask the book to show me what I need to see and then the book opens to those pages. However, I know other practitioners who love computer symbolism, and when they seek out the Akashic records, they visualize a computer where they type in what they seek and the answer pops up on the screen, like an astral plane google search. There are many other ways to visualize these records as well.

53 Edgar Cayce's A.R.E., "Edgar Cayce on the Akashic Records."

EXERCISE: Visit to the Akashic Records

Before visiting the Akashic records, you must have a question in mind. These records are not something you simply scroll or flip through. You need focus and direction. Without that focus, you are likely to receive information that makes no sense, isn't meant for you, or holds no meaning for you.

You can ask the Akashic records about your health or for specific steps on how to improve your health. You can ask the records about your past lives. You can ask about your spiritual allies. You can ask about your career or love life. Anything you want to know about this life or any of the others you have lived can be accessed, so be clear on what you are seeking.

Needs

A recording of the journey

Thirty minutes of uninterrupted time

A clear idea of what you are seeking in the Akashic records

Journal and pen

The Journey

Allow yourself to relax. Take three long, deep cleansing breaths, allowing any tension or distractions to simply be released on the breath. (*Pause here.*)

Continue to breathe slowly and with intention. Allow yourself to sink into where you are sitting. Allow each breath to be an expansion of your form and spirit.

As you breathe, see before you a downward-spiraling staircase. Allow yourself to begin to step down, one step after the other, moving down, down, down this staircase. As you follow the stairs downward, step-by-step, you notice that there are torches on the walls that light up as you approach. You continue to take one step and then another, spiraling down, down, down this winding staircase. Down and down the stairs continue, and you follow them step-by-step, moving ever farther down this staircase. (*Pause here.*)

The torches light up and reveal that you are almost to the bottom of the staircase. Step-by-step, one foot after the other, you reach the bottom of the winding staircase, and in front of you stands a big door. On the other side of this door is the hall of Akashic records. Take a moment to notice what this door looks like. What do you notice about the doorknob? What about any design? (*Pause here.*)

Hold your question in your heart and mind. Be clear about what it is you are seeking in the Akashic records. When you feel ready, knock three times on this door and open it.

Inside you will see the full hall of records. Take in the details of this hall. It will appear slightly different for each of us. What does this library look like for you?

As you step deeper into the hall of records, you see before you a large table. Suddenly a large book appears on the table and opens to the specific page that reveals the answer to your question. Look at the book. The answer might be in words, pictures, images, feelings, or something else altogether. Take some time with the book and see what information comes through. (*Long pause here.*)

When you feel ready, thank the hall of Akashic records and close the book. Turn around and exit through the doorway that brought you here. The door will close behind you. You can return to this place at any time, but for now, begin your ascent back up the spiral staircase that brought you to the hall of records.

Step-by-step, one foot after the other, you move up, up, up these stairs. The torches on the wall turn off after you pass by them. Move up, up, up this spiral staircase until you begin to feel your physical body. Begin to shift your energy, focusing once again on your breath and body.

Once again, breathe slowly and with intention. Focus on feeling your body and returning to the world. When you feel ready, slowly open your eyes and look around your space. Take some time to write down anything important or interesting that came up.

Conclusion

Spirit and magic go hand in hand. I would go so far as to say you can't have one without the other. When working magic, you are tapping into the realm of Spirit. Having respect for the power of magic will only enhance your connection to Spirit.

Chapter 6

SPIRIT HERBS AND BOTANICALS

Traditionally, herbs and botanicals are categorized according to the four elements. For example, cinnamon is an herb of Fire, alfalfa is an herb of Earth, dandelion is an herb of Air, and thyme is an herb of Water.[54] There are hundreds of years of information on herbs and their elemental alignments. Most of this information does not include Spirit as one of the elements.

Even if plants, herbs, trees, and botanicals don't have a traditional alignment with Spirit, there are plenty of them that can help you engage with higher levels of consciousness, psychic abilities, prophetic dreaming, and the like.

The herbs and botanicals listed here are all connected to Spirit, as they can help you connect with psychic skills and spiritual energies and reach higher planes and higher realms of existence.

Spirit Herbs

As you read on, remember not to work with any herb that you are allergic to or that could be harmful or poisonous. If you aren't sure about a possible allergic reaction, it's better to simply not use

54 Cunningham, *Cunningham's Encyclopedia of Magical Herbs.*

the herb in question. There are a couple of herbs in this list that are marked poisonous. They are listed here for informational purposes only and should not be used in any form.

African Violet (Saintpaulia ionantha)

When grown inside the home, African violets help to increase psychic abilities and intuition.

Althea (Althea officinalis)

Althea is known to call in good spirits. When used as an incense or in a sachet, it can help to increase psychic power.

Bay Laurel (Laurus nobilis)

The leaves of this plant can be chewed on or slept on top of to bring prophetic messages. A common magical ritual involves writing a wish on a bay leaf and then burning it. As the smoke rises, feel the wish coming true.

Beech (Fagus sylvatica)

If you carve a wish into a stick of beech wood and bury it, your wish will come true.

Bistort (Polygonum bistorta)

Burning bistort in combination with frankincense will help to increase psychic powers and success with divination.

Borage (Borago officinalis)

Drinking a tea of borage flowers will help to increase your psychic abilities.

Buchu (Barosma betulina)

Burning a small amount of buchu mixed with frankincense right before going to sleep and/or drinking an herbal infusion will bring forth prophetic dreams.

Celery (Apium graveolens)

Burning the seeds of this plant along with orris root will help to increase psychic powers.

Cinnamon (Cinnamomum zeylanicum)

To increase psychic powers, burn some cinnamon as incense, specifically when performing divination.

Citron (Citrus medica)

Eating the citron fruit will aid in increasing psychic abilities.

Dandelion (Taraxacum officinale)

After drying and roasting dandelion roots, make a tea. This will aid in growing psychic abilities and call in good spirits.

Eyebright (Euphrasia officinalis)

Carry a piece of eyebright to help you see the truth and open up your powers of foresight.

Frankincense (Boswellia carterii)

Burning frankincense will bring about visions and can also aid in the process of meditation. Put frankincense in a sachet to help increase your spiritual awareness.

Gum Arabic (Acacia senegal)

Add gum arabic to any type of incense to increase good energy.

Hazel (Corylus cornuta)

Eat hazelnuts before performing divination to help increase your psychic sight. Create a crown of hazel branches and place it on your head, then make a wish, holding a clear focus on your goal. Toss the crown into a fire once you've made the wish for it to come true.

Heliotrope (Heliotropium europaeum)

To increase prophetic dreams, place some heliotrope flowers under your pillow before going to sleep. Warning: This plant is poisonous, so don't imbibe it in any way.

Holly (Ilex aquifolium)

Planting holly around your home will protect you from magical workers who may mean you harm. This is also an excellent plant to wish upon. In total silence, gather nine holly leaves. Wrap the leaves in a white cloth and tie the ends together with nine knots. Put this bundle under your pillow and your dreams will manifest.

Honeysuckle (Lonicera caprifolium)

Crush some honeysuckle flowers and rub them on your forehead to help increase your psychic abilities. This is best done before a divination reading.

Huckleberry (Vaccinium myrtillus)

Carrying this plant or putting it in a sachet will help to increase your luck. Burning it before going to sleep at night will help your dreams manifest.

Kava Kava (Piper methysticum)

Allow this herb to steep in water overnight. Upon rising, drink the kava kava infusion to increase your psychic visions.

Mace (Myristica fragrans)

Mace is actually the outer covering of a nutmeg seed. When burning, it increases psychic powers.

Marigold (Calendula officinalis)

Garlands of marigolds placed over your bed will bring on prophetic dreams.

Mastic (Pistacia lentiscus)

Burning mastic will help to manifest spirits. It is also used to increase psychic abilities and will add potency to any other spellwork you add it to.

Mugwort (Artemisia vulgaris)

Create a small pillow of dried mugwort to help bring on prophetic dreams. Burning this herb or drinking a tea of it will increase psychic powers, especially before performing divination.

Myrrh (Commiphora myrrha)

Myrrh resin will increase the power of anything you use it with. When burned, it will purify the area and help to lift the spirits of those in the space.

Peppermint (Mentha × piperita)

Placing fresh peppermint on your altar will help to call on good spirits and aid in magic. Smelling the herb before bed can encourage prophetic dreaming.

Pipsissewa (Chimaphila umbellata)

When crushed and burned, pipsissewa calls on good spirits to help with spells and other magical workings.

Pomegranate (Punica granatum)

It is believed that if you make a wish before eating pomegranate seeds, your wish will always come true. Branches of the tree hung above entryways will guard against negative energy.

Rowan (Sorbus acuparia)

Carrying a piece of rowan with you will help to increase psychic powers. Burning the leaves and berries will do the same.

Star Anise (Illicum verum)

Wearing star anise seeds or burning them as incense will help to increase psychic powers.

Stillingia (Stillingia sylvatica)

Burning stillingia roots will help to increase psychic abilities. You can use the smoke to help you find lost items. The smoke will move toward the item you ask it to find.

Thyme (Thymus vulgaris)

Wearing thyme will help to increase your psychic skills and also aid you in being able to see the otherworlds, including the faerie realm.

Tonka (Dipteryx odorata)

Dried tonka beans are known to make wishes come true. Hold a dried tonka bean in your dominant hand as you stand near a body of water. Make a wish and then toss the bean into the water.

Uva Ursi (Arctostaphylos uva-ursi)

Adding uva ursi to a sachet will increase psychic abilities.

Walnut (Juglans regia)

If you ever receive a bag of walnuts as a gift, it means that all your wishes will come true.

Wormwood (Artemisia absinthium)

Burning wormwood in a cemetery will raise the dead. Warning: This plant is poisonous, so don't imbibe it in any way.

Spirit Incense, Oils, and Baths

Spirit herbs are just the first step in delving into the world of herbs and the element of Spirit. Creating your own incense blends, bath mixes, teas, and oils is an amazing way to connect more deeply with herbs in general. When you get your hands dirty and really have a tactile experience of the herbs, it will serve your magic so much more.

Spirit Incense Blends

To create an incense blend, use the dried herbs. Grind them as much as you can and then blend them together. These blends can be placed on top of an incense charcoal to burn. Always make sure to follow fire safety precautions!

Calling Spirits Incense

Burn this incense when you want to call spirits into your space.

2 parts coriander
2 parts mugwort
1 part camphor
1 part flax
1 part anise

Divination Incense

Burn this incense while performing divination. You can also use this smoke to cleanse your divination tools.

1 part clove
1 part orange peel
1 part cinnamon
1 part cinquefoil

Prophecy Incense

Burn this incense for psychic work or before bedtime to bring prophetic dreams.

2 parts frankincense
1 part parsley

Psychic Incense

Burn this incense to help strengthen your psychic abilities.

1 part frankincense
1 part cinnamon
1 part clove
Several drops orange oil

Spirit Incense

Burn this incense any time you want to call on Spirit as an element for guidance or information.

2 parts mugwort
1 part borage
1 part dandelion
1 part thyme

Spirit Oil Blends

To create an oil blend, start with the essential oils. Mix these together first and then add them to a carrier oil. Essential oils need to be diluted in a carrier oil; otherwise they are too strong and can burn the skin or cause allergic reactions. In a half ounce of carrier oil, you should have no more than thirty drops of essential oil. Your carrier oil should be as bland as possible so it doesn't interfere with your essential oils. Grapeseed oil and almond oil are good options.

Astral Travel Oil

Use this oil on your pulse points when you are going to astral travel.

5 drops sandalwood
1 drop ylang-ylang
1 drop cinnamon
1 drop myrrh

Psychic Oil

Wear this oil when you want to increase your psychic vision. It works well for scrying and can be used to anoint crystals for scrying purposes.

5 drops lemongrass
1 drop yarrow
1 drop mugwort

Spirit Baths

To make a Spirit bath, start with a mixture of one part kosher salt, one part Epsom salt, and one part coarse salt. Add the suggested herbs and oils to the salts. Mix well and add at least one large scoop to a hot bath. Use dried herbs and grind them down into a fine powder.

Divination Bath

Use this bath blend before performing divination to help open your psychic abilities.

3 parts thyme
3 parts rose
1 part nutmeg
10 drops patchouli oil

Psychic Bath

Use this bath blend when you want to increase your psychic skills. The more often you use it, the more effective it will be.

3 parts lemongrass
3 parts thyme
2 parts orange peel
5 drops clove oil

Spirit Teas

Creating a tea is one of the best ways to work with Spirit and herbs. With tea, you can literally imbibe the energy of the herbs. The best way to work with tea is to mix the dried herbs together and then pour hot water over the top of them. Let the herbs steep for about ten minutes, strain the herbs, and drink. You can drink the tea and/or breathe in the steam of the tea to start the process. You can also add a sweetener to the tea if you prefer.

Clairvoyance Tea

This tea will help open your third eye and allow you to develop the skill of foresight.

3 parts rose
1 part cinnamon
1 part mugwort

Psychic Tea

Drink this tea while performing divination to help your psychic skills stay strong and open.

3 parts rose
2 parts hibiscus
1 part yarrow

Conclusion

On top of the connection between Spirit and plants, there is also the individual spirit of a plant. While working with Spirit, you are connecting with the large Spirit of plants, but you can also connect with the individual spirit of each plant, like the basil in your window or the bushes in your yard. Plants have spirits just like humans do, and we can feel into these energies when we grow them or even just sit by them.

Chapter 7

SPIRIT CRYSTALS AND STONES

There are so many stones that can help you connect more deeply with the element of Spirit. The stones that help you raise your vibration, connect with the higher realms, and aid in meditation are all great stones for Spirit.

When working with stones, it's best if you can have them on your skin. Contact with the skin helps you get the most of the stone's healing energy. Tucking a stone in your pocket or carrying it with you is the next best step. And if all else fails, having the stone in a location where you can see it or creating an altar with stones will help boost the energy you want to work with.

The best way to know if a stone or crystal is right for you or the work you are embarking on is to hold it in your hand and see if it feels right. It is so important to obtain your stones in person. This might involve going to a mine and getting your own stones right out of the earth, or going to a gem fair and talking to the folks who obtained the stones. It could also be going to a crystal shop and finding the right stone. Having a physical opportunity with any stone will give you the best information.

CHAPTER 7

Spirit Stones

The following list of Spirit stones is just a jumping-off point. Remember, connecting crystals and stones with the element of Spirit is a rather personal process. Figure out what works for you.

Ametrine

Ametrine is a combination of amethyst and citrine. It helps to connect the physical world to the spirit realms and is an excellent stone to use for protection when astral traveling. This stone can help you clear your mind for meditation. It helps to clear negative energy from the body and can help strengthen the immune system and clear blockages.

Angelite

Angelite can help facilitate connection and communication with the angelic realms and increase telepathic powers and psychic abilities. This is a stone of compassion, helping to transform pain into healing. When these stones are applied to the feet, they help to clear the body's energetic pathways.

Apophyllite

Apophyllite helps us connect to the power of the Akashic records. It can help to raise the energy of any place where it stands. It is a protector when you are having an out-of-body or astral experience. It is a stone of truth, for both seeing and speaking the truth. This is an excellent stone to use in energy healing.

Azurite

Azurite is used for psychic and intuitive abilities and can aid in astral and spirit travel. This stone can be used when stepping into channeling. Azurite is used to help clear old programmed beliefs and shift into a more positive state of being. It helps to clear the mind and relieve stress.

Celestite

Celestite is known for helping us connect with the angelic realms. It is a stone of divine energy and high vibration. Celestite can help you remember your dreams and strengthen your clairvoyant abilities. It is a healing stone, known to heal the aura and bring in balance. Placing it on the point of the third eye will open up that energy center and help you connect to universal energy.

Charoite

Often called the stone of transformation, charoite is considered a soul stone. It encourages change and helps to raise vibration. This stone can help you release negativity and fears. It can help you bring your spiritual self more into the present moment and connect with messages from past lives.

Danburite

Danburite is a highly spiritual stone connected to the heart's power. It is known for connecting higher consciousness with the power of the talking self, giving you more self-awareness. Holding this stone while in meditation will allow you to move between realms more easily. Known for stimulating the third eye, danburite can help increase peace and awareness.

Iolite

Iolite is connected to the power of the third eye and can help with traveling between the worlds. It can clear negative thoughts and help you express your true feelings. Iolite can also help with relationship communication, allowing the truth to be said and heard with an open heart.

Kyanite

Kyanite can help with meditation. It is known to amplify energy and increase psychic abilities. This stone can help you connect with your spirit guides and open up communication with the other realms. This is a dream stone, helping you to remember dreams and also have prophetic dreams. Kyanite won't hold negative energy and doesn't require cleansing. It can help with truth and clarity.

Lapis Lazuli

Lapis lazuli is known to help open up the power of the third eye. It can aid in dreamwork and increase psychic abilities. This is a stone of deep peace and profound connection, removing stress and clearing out blocks. Lapis lazuli is also known as a reversal stone, sending any negative energy back to its source. It is a harmonizing stone that can reveal inner truths and clear anger.

Larimar

Known for helping people connect to alternate dimensions, larimar is a highly spiritual stone. It is spiritually empowering, aiding in angelic communication and meditation. This stone can pull off negative attachments, including entities that are stuck in the aura. Larimar can aid us in reconnecting with nature and the energy of the earth.

Merlinite

Merlinite is known for helping people connect with the Akashic records. It is often referred to as the stone of shamans because it can help us shift between the realms. This stone can aid you in creating successful rituals. If you want to bring more magic into your life, this is a must-have stone.

Moldavite

Moldavite comes from a meteorite that fell to the earth millions of years ago. It is extremely rare and can help you connect to the extraterrestrial realms. Moldavite is a very high-vibration stone that helps people connect with the Divine and the spirit realms. This stone will connect you with the highest spiritual planes, including accessing the Akashic records.

Petalite

Petalite is an angelic stone with a high vibration. It can aid in meditation while offering protection. This stone can help to heal family trauma going back generations. When you are seeking answers from the other realms, this stone can aid in that process. Petalite can help you leap forward in the development of your spiritual skills, increasing your abilities with ease.

Phenacite

Phenacite is a stone with one of the highest vibrations. It connects to the angelic realms and can help us access the Akashic records. This stone will help bring high spiritual energy into the earthly realms. Even though it is a high-vibration stone, it has a subtle power. Phenacite has the power to amplify the power of other stones.

Phantom Quartz

A quartz crystal with an internal shadow is called a phantom quartz. Known for aiding in personal and planetary healing, this stone can help us access the Akashic records and connect with energy from past lives. This stone can help to open powers of *clairaudience*, or being able to "hear" the voices from other realms.

Seraphinite

As you might be able to tell by its name, seraphinite is a stone of angelic wisdom. This is a stone of spiritual enlightenment and the energy of the crown chakra. It is a stone of high vibration, aiding in realm travel and meditation.

Stilbite

Stilbite helps to open up intuitive skills. If working with your intuition is new to you, this stone can help. It is a highly metaphysical stone and can aid in meditation. A high-vibration stone, stilbite can aid in scrying and in any type of spiritual journey, especially in the higher spiritual realms.

Unakite

Unakite is a third eye stone, also referred to as a stone of vision. Known to support emotional and spiritual growth, unakite can aid in psychic visions. It is an excellent scrying stone and can aid in integration. Unakite brings in calm energy. It is a rebirthing stone, helping to clear blockages from the past.

Spirit Stone Elixirs

A stone elixir is water that has been charged with the energy of a stone or crystal. It is another way to take the energy or spirit of a stone or crystal into your body. A stone elixir can be used as a room spray, added to a bath to cleanse the body, or ingested as a drink (as long as you know the stone is safe to work with in this manner). You can add the elixir to teas or other forms of spellwork to increase that spell's energy.

Before creating an elixir, make sure you research the stone or crystal that you want to use. Many stones, such as apophylite, are toxic or can be damaged by water.

The following stones are safe for making elixirs. Before starting, check the stones for cracks, because the elixir process can break stones that are already damaged.

- Amethyst elixir: can help with sleep issues. It is also good for protection and can be sprayed around doorways to help with protection spells.
- Blue agate elixir: can help bring clarity to communication. Spray it on the throat chakra or in a room before or after a difficult conversation.
- Carnelian elixir: can help increase energy and motivation. Use this at the office or when there's a project that needs to be completed.
- Clear quartz elixir: known to aid in anything you ask it to. Clear quartz can be used for any type of elixir you desire. Just program the stone for what you want.
- Rose quartz elixir: is perfect for keeping relationships smooth or for calling new love into your life. This type of elixir can also aid in improving self-love.
- Smoky quartz elixir: is great to use when you need to feel secure or be brought back down to earth.

EXERCISE: Create an Elixir

Here are the general directions for making a stone elixir.

Needs

6–12 tumbled chips of the stone of your choice

Pot of distilled or spring water

Bowl of salt and distilled or spring water

A blue or amber bottle with a spray top

High-percentage alcohol (Apple cider vinegar can be used if alcohol is not suitable.)

Directions

Once you have picked your stones, the first step is to clean them. Start with soap and water. Scrub the stones to remove any excess dirt or residue. Once the stones are rinsed free of soap, place them in a pot of distilled or spring water and boil them for three to five minutes. Once they are cool, place them in a bowl of salt and distilled or spring water for forty-five minutes.

Place your stones in the blue or amber bottle and fill it three-quarters of the way full with distilled or spring water. Then fill the bottle to the top with a high-percentage alcohol, such as vodka. If alcohol is a no-go for you, you can substitute apple cider vinegar. The alcohol/vinegar allows the elixir to stay potent longer. Store the elixir in a cool, dry place and use it as needed.

Spray your elixir in a room or over your head to shift the energy in the space. Don't spray in your eyes.

If you haven't used the full elixir after three months, pour the remains out onto the earth at a new moon. If you want more of the same elixir, you will need to make a fresh batch.

• • • •

The Spirit of Water

Lilith Dorsey (New York, NY) comes from a Celtic, Afro-Caribbean, and Native American spirituality. She is the editor and publisher of *Oshun-African Magickal Quarterly*, filmmaker of the documentary *Bodies of Water: Voodoo Identity and Tranceformation*, cohost of the YouTube show *Witchcraft*

& Voodoo, and author of *Voodoo and Afro-Caribbean Paganism* (Citadel, 2005), *Orishas, Goddesses, and Voodoo Queens* (Weiser, 2020), and *Water Magic* (Llewellyn, 2020).

The Spirit of Water is everywhere. In fact, our bodies are made up mostly of water. Water is also all around us, as the earth is made up of mostly water. Humans and nearly everything else on our planet depend on water to survive. Water can be gentle, like the morning dew, or terrifying, like a tidal wave.

Many practitioners rely on water as a necessary part of their spiritual practice. This can be something as simple as a glass of water left out for your ancestors next to their photo or a more complicated magickal bath used to cleanse the spirit of the negativity that can surround us at times.

I have been an initiated practitioner of the African Traditional Religions of New Orleans Voodoo, Haitian Vodou, and La Regla Lucumi (also known as Santeria) for over three decades. In these traditions, all forms of water are sacred and resonate with their own unique character. For example, river water is said to embody the energy of the orisha, or divinity, known as Oshún in the religion of La Regla Lucumi. She holds the power to heal issues of fertility, problems in love, and struggles with money or finances. If at all possible, offerings to her are to be brought directly to the river to humbly ask for her guidance and direction.

When crafting altars or shrines for Oshún, river water is almost always present. The same is true when crafting ritual baths, floorwashes, and spellwork for her. For those unfamiliar with African Traditional Religions, the fact that this orisha not only is honored with river water but also is seen as being present in that water may be difficult to grasp. Everywhere there is river water this sacred energy is present. Other traditions assign specific gods or goddesses as the spirit of specific rivers.

In London, the River Thames has been associated with an ancient deity called Tamesis and also the Egyptian goddess Isis. The famous river in Paris, the Seine, is said to be connected to a nymph named Sequana, who was said to reside in the springs there, according to Gallic mythology. My hometown of New Orleans honors the sacred Mississippi River as being the site of African orishas such as Oshún and Yemayá and also a folk heroine known as Annie Christmas.

It is easy for those who wish to connect with the spirit of Water to learn more about any of these goddesses and inspirational figures. This process can be done in an educational way or in an experiential way, by creating altars for them or finding an inspirational piece of art to meditate with while thinking about the true nature of Water in all its glory.

Alternatively, people may wish to seek the true manifestation of the spirit of Water by going to the source. This process can be sublime. Sitting by the water's edge and feeling and listening to the messages that come on a deep level is one way to access some of this spiritual power. Another way would be to leave a biodegradable offering of flowers or food at the water's edge and ask the spirit of the place if it would be okay to take a small amount of water to use in your magick. Remember to abide by all local laws and guidelines. When you get home, a drop of this water can be added to your magickal baths, floor washes, and the like. Notice what effect this addition has on you, honor it, and try to internalize it as best you can.

There are probably as many ways to connect with the spirit of Water as there are drops in the ocean. My best advice is to keep searching until you find one or more ways that work for you.

Water is a vital element, and living in harmony with the spirit of it will always bring deep power.

Lilith Dorsey

• • • •

Conclusion

Stones, crystals, and gems hold the Spirit of the earth within them, but the way this Spirit manifests is unique to each stone. The Spirit of stones can help you connect to the higher realms. It can help you remember your own god-self and your spiritual body.

Chapter 8

SPIRIT ANIMAL GUIDES

Spirit animal guides are the big energies of an animal. Rather than working with the spirit of the cat that lives in your house, we are talking about the Spirit of Cat. This is the big energy of that animal. Cryptids and mythological creatures are all animal guides of Spirit. You can refer back to chapter 2 for more information on mythological creatures and how to work with them.

The animals of Spirit are those of liminal spaces. They may be found on the edges or boundaries. These animals are of the in-between spaces. They may fit into more than one realm or element.

The animals of Spirit are those known to be messengers. They are the animals connected to the other realms, the psychopomps and messengers for cultures across the world. If you find yourself drawn to an animal of Spirit, it could take some time for that relationship to develop. Spiritual allies come to us for a reason, a season, or a lifetime.

You might have a powerful interaction with an animal that happens only once. It could take place out in the world or in a dream. This is a spiritual message that is meant for one moment and it can be fleeting, with the animal spirit moving on as soon as the message is received.

You might find yourself drawn to an animal for just a short moment. It may be that there is an animal whose energy is one you would like to emulate in your life. Perhaps that animal possesses attributes you would like to possess, so you work with them as a spiritual ally. Once you feel secure in that power, you might find yourself distancing yourself from that animal. This is the animal of a potential season.

Then there are those spiritual allies that stick around for your whole life, where you work on that relationship and learn from that animal all the time.

Spirit Animal Guides

Here is a list of animals that are known to carry important messages and what their energies mean for difficult cultures. There are so many more animals that could be on this list. If there is a Spirit animal that you feel connected to, that is what is really important. The Spirit animals listed here are mainly ones of liminal ties, but any animal has the potential to be connected to Spirit.

You may feel an affinity with an animal but have no physical relationship with it. You may feel a kinship with one of these animals even if you've never even seen one in the flesh.

Bee

Generally speaking, in every culture where bees are native, they are a positive omen. They are a symbol of community. The way that bees work together is a powerful reminder that humans also need to work together for the overall health of the species. In some folklore, bees are a symbol of wealth and abundance. There are traditions that say that killing a bee will bring bad luck. Even as far back as ancient Egypt, bees were revered.

There is evidence that the first artificial hives made by human hands were in Egypt. The ancient Egyptians even referred to honey as liquid gold, and honey has been found in tombs, still edible thousands of years later. Honey has been used to treat burns, aid in healing sore throats, and clear up other skin conditions. Honeycombs are constructed in a hexagonal shape, which is a geometrical shape connected to the mystical. The six-sided structure is often a symbol of the heart and the sun.

Bees are animals of Spirit because they are pollinators and they work with the land and the sky. They work with humans, helping our fruit and vegetables to grow.[55]

Butterfly

The transformative power of the butterfly cannot be matched by any other creature on earth. The being known as a caterpillar spends its entire existence eating and eating and eating. When it can eat no more, it transforms itself into a cocoon and dissolves into a goo. From the goo, it redevelops into a butterfly. How amazing! We can't possibly know what that process feels like, but in my imagination it's gotta be hard.

In many traditions, butterflies are symbols of transformation, hope, and joy. When butterflies flit from one flower to another, they can look like they are dancing, and that is part of their message: to find joy in our everyday activities. For many, butterflies are messengers from the beloved dead.

The butterfly is an animal of Spirit because of the transformation process it goes through in order to exist. Before emerging as a butterfly, it becomes a liminal being, melting down totally.[56]

55 Andrews, *Animal Speak*, 337.

56 Andrews, *Animal Speak*, 339–40.

Cat

There may be no witchier animal on earth than the cat. Cats have a long association with Witches in folklore and mythology. They are considered a domesticated animal, which means we have invited them into our homes and we feed and take care of them; but of all the domesticated animals, cats are still pretty feral—this is their relationship to Spirit. They are a part of our human society, but they are their own animal. Cats have been revered in ancient cultures across traditions. In ancient Egypt, cats were honored. Wealthy Egyptians would have their cats mummified with them at death to spend time with them in the afterlife. The Egyptian goddess Bastet is pictured with the head of a cat. In Norse myth, the goddess Freya drives a chariot pulled by two cats. In Hinduism, the goddess of childbirth is seen riding on a cat. The myth and folklore around cats is often contradictory. They are seen as clever and maybe even a little devious. They are both feared and beloved. Cats see well in the dark, and for a domesticated animal, they can do just fine without the intervention of humans in their lives.[57]

Crow or Raven

Although crows and ravens are different creatures, they are related and much of the mythology and folklore surrounding these birds crosses over. In Greek myth, crows started out as white birds, but after they brought Apollo bad news, he turned them all black in his anger. In Norse myth, Odin has two ravens, Hugin and Munin, which translate in English to "thought" and "memory." They are Odin's watchers and bring him information on world happenings every night. Crows are also known as watchers,

57 Andrews, *Animal Speak*, 258–59.

and their communities will set a sentinel to watch for trouble or potential threats.

Crows and ravens both have complex language skills and communicate with one another using a set of caws, clicks, and other noises. There are ravens that can speak and understand English! Because they are clever, they pay attention to the easiest sources of food and are known to steal from other birds. In Celtic myth, crows are part of the creation legends; this is also true for the Athabascan people of Alaska. In Chinese myth, a crow with three legs is connected to the sun and to solitude. The raven was one of the birds that flew off from Noah's Ark and didn't return. In the Pacific Northwest Indigenous communities, Raven is a trickster that helped save the sun. In Irish myth, ravens are connected to the goddess of war and battle, the Morrigan. The crow or raven is an animal of Spirit because in many cultures it is seen as a messenger from the other realms.[58]

Deer

Deer can be found on every continent except Australia, so it's no surprise that they show up in the folklore and mythos of so many different peoples. In some tales, deer are creatures of the otherworlds, luring powerful men to get lost in the woods. The story of Sir Gawain is one of these stories, where the knight gets lost in the woods after following a white hart (white being a sign that the creature is likely from the otherworld). Buddha is often depicted as a deer, and there is a message of gentleness that goes along with this imagery. As a symbol of the other realms, the deer is naturally an animal of Spirit. A deer's antlers get bigger every year and they sit just behind the eyes on the head. This is a sign of the animal having a connection to higher realms and being able to "see" what

58 Andrews, *Animal Speak*, 130–32, 187–88.

isn't in front of us. There is an energy of gentleness and softness that a deer brings. They have heightened hearing and are always on alert. Deers also have an amazing jump. They can go from standing still to leaping over a nine-foot fence with ease.[59]

Dragonfly

Dragonflies are one of the more ancient creatures still alive on the planet, making their first appearance millions of years ago. These insects can fly over thirty miles an hour and they move in all directions. Some myths have said that the dragonfly moves light itself. Dragonflies are creatures of water and air. They lay their eggs in the water and spend their early life stages in the water before taking flight. This offers a unique ability to connect with thought and emotion. As an animal of Spirit, they have a relationship to multiple elements and are able to move in multiple directions in mid-flight. In Japanese folklore, they represent light. For the Native American Zuni, the dragonfly has supernatural powers. In many Eastern European cultures, the dragonfly is associated with Witches, and not in a good way. In Sweden, there are folktales of dragonflies sewing the lips of naughty children together. They were often referred to as water Witches or the devil's horses.[60]

Fox

Is it a dog? Is it a cat? No, the fox is some secret third thing. These creatures mesmerize humans because they look like man's best friend but behave like a trickster cat. There are twelve species of what are considered "true" foxes and they are found in a wide range of climates. Foxes are liminal beings. They are most active at dawn and dusk and tend to live on the edges of wild and culti-

59 Andrews, *Animal Speak*, 262–64.
60 Brenner, "Folklore & Nature: Dragonflies."

vated lands. Liminality is connected to the fae realms or the other-worlds, and the fox is very much an emissary of these places. There are folk stories of foxes being able to shape-shift into human form, and their calls sound like a woman screaming. One of their greatest skills is to camouflage themselves, hiding in plain sight. This is another nod to their liminal energy. Foxes will also "charm" their prey. They will prance and dance and roll around to get the attention of something they are hunting. When their prey is distracted by their charm, they pounce. This is trickster energy at its finest. In Japanese folklore, the kitsune is a mythical fox, often with many tales and the ability to shape-shift.[61]

Frog

Frogs are liminal beings, able to exist on land and in water. In many cultures they are connected to rain and being able to bring on the rains. Because of this relationship with rain and water, they are believed to help people deal with heavy emotions, grief, and deep sadness. Rains will also bring frogs out from their hibernation on the land, which can make it seem like they are coming from the rain itself. In ancient Egypt, the goddess Heket, sometimes spelled Heqit, was often pictured with the head of a frog. She was called upon to assist women during pregnancy and labor. In pre-Columbian Mesoamerica, there were many tribes that worshipped a goddess named Centeotl, who was a protector of pregnant women. She was seen in the form of a frog with many udders.[62] There is a deep correlation between fertility, pregnancy, and frogs. The Maori people of New Zealand believe that killing a frog can lead to heavy rains and flooding.

61 Andrews, *Animal Speak*, 271–77.
62 Exploratorium. "Frog Myths."

Hummingbird

Hummingbirds fly by moving their wings in a figure-eight pattern. This shape is also known as the infinity symbol, which connects this wee little bird to the astral realms. These birds are unable to walk; however, they are the most skilled fliers of any other birds in the world, being able to move in any direction. It is this air skill that makes them an animal of Spirit. Hummingbirds can fly very fast and then come to a complete stop, seeming to float in midair. Because of their high energy, they also need to eat a lot. They will eat up to sixty times a day. These birds are also constantly in play; it may look like they are fighting with each other or battling it out, but they are just playing, as these birds never actually harm each other when the "fighting" starts. They go into a deep sleep state called torpor overnight and fly great distances. The ancient Mayans believed that hummingbirds were the sun god in disguise. In hoodoo there is a magickal oil blend called Chuparrosa, which is the Spanish name for hummingbird. It is believed to bring in love and sweetness in romance.[63]

Owl

Owls can be an omen of death or a symbol of wisdom depending on the culture that is looking at it. Part of this conflict is likely due to the fact that owls are nocturnal creatures and have large eyes that seem to look into the very soul. In ancient Greece, the owl was connected to the goddess Athena, who ruled over wisdom and strategy. The owl is connected to the ancient entity known at Lilith. Her original name was Lilitu, which translates to owl. In several Native American tribes, the owl is a sign of death or a symbol of the realm of the dead. An owl's flight is silent; it can move

63 Andrews, *Animal Speak*, 157–59.

with a stealth that is not really matched by any other animal. In ancient Rome, owls were believed to be Witches in disguise who would suck the blood of babies. All over the world, the owl is seen as wisdom and/or death, which makes a lot of sense if you think about death being the last lesson that we will learn. It is their relationship to the dead and wisdom that gives owls their powerful connection to Spirit.[64]

Rabbit

Rabbits are often seen as being from the otherworlds or as liminal beings, which is what gives them the connection to Spirit.[65] They have a rapid gestation cycle, being able to have babies two to five times a year, so it's no wonder that in many cultures they are associated with fertility. Rabbits are active at any time of day or night, but they are most often seen at dusk or dawn, which connects them with liminal time. In China, the rabbit is one of the astrological signs. Those born in a Rabbit year are known to be artistic and sensitive. Rabbit is quick and clever and can jump to amazing heights. For the Celtic people, rabbits were a sign of abundance, and it was considered taboo to eat them. There are many stories of Druids releasing rabbits and watching them run as a means of divination. In ancient Greece, rabbits were animals connected to Aphrodite and Eros,[66] so they were seen as a symbol of love. Rabbits were often given as wedding gifts at the time. A modern superstition is to say "rabbit, rabbit, rabbit" on the first day of the month to bring good luck for the days ahead.

64 Andrews, *Animal Speak*, 172–81.
65 Keys, "Hares in Celtic Mythology."
66 Wilkes, "Hares in Roman Art by Isobel Wilkes."

Spider

As you can imagine, the spider shows up in myth in virtually all cultures and often as a weaver of fate or connection. In ancient Greece, the goddess Athena turned Arachne into a spider after she boasted about being the best weaver. In West African myth, Anansi is a trickster spirit and most often shaped like a spider. He is often connected to storytelling and wisdom. In several Native American tribes, Spider is the creator of the world and/or human beings. There is an old folktale in England that finding a spider on your clothing means you will come into money. In Japanese folklore, there is a being that looks like a beautiful woman but actually has a spider body. In ancient Egypt, the goddess Neith was the weaver of fate and was connected to spiders.[67]

Snakes

Snakes are an often misunderstood creature, because in most places in the world there are snakes that are quite dangerous. Snakes are shape-shifters because they shed their skin as they grow bigger. They have no arms or legs and can feel the subtle shifts happening deep in the earth. It can seem like the snake has the widest pendulum swing of beliefs attached to it of virtually any animal. In some cultures the snake is the epitome of evil, and in others it is the ultimate healer. In many Mesoamerican societies, the snake is connected to the feathered god Quetzalcoatl, who is believed to be returning to earth when humans are in great need.[68] In ancient Greece, snakes were connected to healing and the god Hermes was seen carrying a staff with two snakes winding around it. This symbol is called the caduceus and is still the symbol for modern medicine. In Chinese astrology, the snake is one of the twelve signs.

67 Wigington, "Spider Mythology and Folklore."
68 Pruitt, "9 Powerful Snakes from History and Mythology."

People born in the year of the Snake are believed to be clever and charming and have the gift of clairvoyance. In ancient Egypt, the snake was a symbol of foresight and being able to divine what is ahead. The snake eating its own tail is the ouroboros and is a symbol of death, resurrection, and rebirth.

Turtles

Turtles are a sacred animal in virtually all regions where they live. The continent of North America is called Turtle Island by many Native communities, where the mythos is that a giant turtle carries the land on its back. Turtles can live on land or in water and often spend a lot of time on the shoreline. This is a liminal space, which connects them with the otherworld. Turtles live long lives and their mythos often connects them with longevity. In Hawaiian myth, turtles are symbols of good luck and strength. The ancient Hawaiians used the shells of certain turtles as currency. During the Shang Dynasty in China, turtle shells were used as a form of divination and the animal was seen as a symbol of strength and health.[69]

Vulture

The vulture shows up in Greek myth as a descendant of the mythical griffin. For the Assyrians, the god of death would show up in the guise of a vulture. In ancient Egypt, the vulture was connected to the goddess Isis, who was a great healer. Greeks and Romans would use parts of the vulture as talismans for healing. Some cultures around the Mediterranean region believed that all vultures were female and reproduced by parthenogenesis. Vultures are scavengers and literally help clean up sites where animals have

69 Muse Spells, "Turtles in Mythology."

died. For this reason, they are often connected to the cycles of death and rebirth.[70]

Working with Spirit Animal Guides

Developing relationships with animal guides is about the same as working with other spiritual beings, the main difference being that with an animal guide you have a very real opportunity to see that being in the corporeal world! That isn't always the case with other types of spiritual guides.

In my early days as a practicing Witch, I was taught that there are two ways to work with animal allies. And after all this time, I still find it to be true. Remember, this isn't about having a deep relationship with your pet rabbit; it's about developing a relationship with the overarching Spirit that is Rabbit.

The first way for an animal relationship to start is with that animal coming to you. This doesn't necessarily mean a fox is going to knock on your door and ask if you want to hang out. But it could mean a fox shows up in your life and it causes a spiritual stirring within you that you want to explore. It's more than seeing a fox and thinking, "Oh wow, a fox! That's cool." When an animal shows up as a sign for you, it can spark a deep knowing that this animal means something more. It is a trusting of your intuition and using that tool of discernment.

The second way for an animal relationship to start is for you to call out to that animal ally. Maybe there is something about the energy of a fox that you desire. Maybe there is something about the power of the fox that you know you need more of in your life.

70 Vulture Conservation Foundation, "The Symbolic Representation of Vultures Across Civilizations—A Review."

This requires you to reach out to that animal. You have to be the one to knock on the door and see what manifests.

It doesn't matter whether that animal shows up or you make the call. Either way, it is your spirit understanding that this energy is needed in your life.

Sometimes an animal guide will show up to deliver one specific message, and once you've received that message they move on. Occasionally I think these are messengers from our other allies to get our attention.

For example, I am scared of spiders. One year when I was away for a week, I came home to discover hundreds (I am not exaggerating here) of baby spiders all over the floor of my bedroom. There was no way I could avoid dealing with them. There was no glass large enough to trap them all. I had to get my hands in there and clear them out of my space.

Spiders carry a message of connectivity and community. That was very much a message I needed at the time. It was shocking and terrifying, but the message was received. This was not a sign for me to start working with spider as an ally; rather, I believe another one of my allies sent spider to deliver the message. Thankfully, it hasn't happened again.

Sometimes an animal guide will show up when you need to shore up your boundaries or face a challenging situation in your life. This ally will show up to help you through it, and once you accomplish the goal they move on. When this happens, I find the animal that shows up has an energy or power that I very much need in my life. When I learn to accept this power or boost it in my life, the ally's work is done and they move on.

But then there are those animal guides that are present in our lives. I've yet to meet someone who hasn't had a connection with some animal or another for most of their lives. Maybe you've always loved elephants, or you've had a "thing" with sharks, or you're obsessed with snakes. A lifelong connection (appreciation, obsession, admiration) can point to a lifelong animal guide. These are beings who signed up with you to help you along your spiritual path. Some folks believe that we have only one true animal guide in our lifetime and the rest are the allies that come and go, but I think it's possible to have multiple lifetime animal guides.

Think back to your childhood. Was there a type of animal that you loved? Was there an animal that you felt connected to or were enamored with? Is there an animal that you loved as a child and still feel a thread of connection to now? These are the places to start looking.

My daughter was born in the spring, and everyone who came to see her brought a little stuffed rabbit. It was springtime and stuffed rabbits were easy to come by, but one person brought her a little stuffed lion. We used to set up all her stuffed toys with the lion in the middle of all the rabbits. I found it hilarious, this one little lion surrounded by rabbits. It almost felt like he was hiding among them, a lion amongst the rabbits. However, as she grew up, my daughter started talking about lions a lot. She always told us that she was a lion. I've maintained that she and lion have life work to do together. Lion is one of her allies.

One animal is not better than any other. If you find yourself called to work with a lion or a mouse, there is power in each of these beings. The perceived ferocity of a creature doesn't mean that its spiritual messages are more powerful. Animal guides are messengers for our spiritual paths. Each relationship will be unique and often exactly what we need.

There is no such thing as a weak animal guide. A mouse and a mountain lion are different beings, and on the surface one might look stronger, but they both have strengths. Plus, when you start working with your animal guides, it's important to look at what they eat and what eats them. Animals exist in a world of reciprocity, give-and-take, prey and predator. When you begin to develop relationships with your guides, you step into that cycle too.

When you start working with an animal ally, look at their entire life. What do they eat? What eats them? Where do they live? How do they live? All these things will offer clues to how to work with them and how their energy might impact your spiritual life.

EXERCISE: Meeting Your Animal Guide

This is a trance meditation to meet an animal ally. Before starting this meditation, be clear about what type of ally you want to meet. Is this a reason, a season, or a lifetime guide that you are seeking out?

With this trance, you can either have someone read it out loud for you or record it and play it back for yourself. As you read the trance, speak slowly and clearly, leaving time and space for the process to unfold without trying to force it.

Do this meditation when you can be undisturbed for at least thirty minutes. Sit or lie down comfortably and allow yourself to just breathe.

Needs

At least thirty minutes of uninterrupted time

Glass of water

Journal and pen

The Journey

Allow your breathing to slow. With each breath, feel into the edges of your body. Allow each breath to come deeper and slower.

Let the breath continue to come in and out slow and easy. As you do, allow for the edges of your body to widen and spread out. Each breath makes it easier for you to widen and soften and get lighter and lighter. Keep this easy, slow breathing going. Slow and easy. (*Pause here.*)

As you breathe and expand, allow your Witch's eye to open. Your Witch's eye is that third eye, the one that sits just above and between your normal seeing eyes. With each breath, this all-knowing eye opens more and more until you see in front of you a winding path.

Let your feet begin to follow this path. Place one foot in front of the other, following along step-by-step. As you walk along the path, take a moment to notice your surroundings. Is there anything interesting or curious along the pathway? Notice what you can smell in the air or hear in the distance. Take a moment to notice the time of day and the weather happening around you.

Step-by-step you keep moving until you come to an opening in the pathway. Step into this opening and take another moment to see what is around you. Feel the air. Smell what is in the air. Take a moment to connect with this open place. (*Pause here.*)

Across from you on the other side of the opening you hear movement. There is a rustling and you can tell that something is headed for you. A creature enters the meadow. It might float or fly. It might slither or walk. It might swim or move in an unpredictable way. But your animal guide moves toward you and becomes ever more clear, firm, and solid as it does.

Your animal guide might be clear and solid or you might just get a sensation of what the guide is. You might also hear the name of the guide or get an idea of it. All these ways of experiencing your guide are valid.

You and your animal guide stand before each other. Take a moment to communicate. This communication might happen with words, sounds, noises, or just overall feelings that come through you. Allow it to unfold. (*Pause here.*)

Ask your animal guide what it wants you to know right now. (*Pause here.*)

Ask your animal guide what symbol you should watch out for when it wants to communicate with you. (*Pause here.*)

Take a moment to say anything else or ask any other questions you are holding in your heart. (*Pause here.*)

If you haven't already, take a moment to thank your animal guide and offer them your gratitude. Say your goodbyes and know that your time here is over, but you can return to this place to visit with your animal guide at any time. (*Pause here.*)

Turn away and walk back to the path that brought you to this opening. Step-by-step, move back along the pathway. As you walk, once again notice your surroundings. Is anything different? Notice what you can see, hear, smell, and feel.

With one foot in front of the other, continue to walk along the pathway. As you do, allow your Witch's eye to return to its normal state of being. Let that Witch's eye, that third eye, begin to gently close. As that eye closes, begin to notice your body. Focus again on your breath. Take some deep breaths and allow your edges to become firmer and more solid.

Take a moment to connect with the edges of your body. Breathe into your feet. Breathe into the top of your head. When you feel ready, slowly open your eyes. If you have been lying down, slowly sit up. Tap the edges of your body and place your hands on the top of your head while you take a deep breath.

When you feel ready, drink a glass of water and write down anything important or interesting that came up for you.

Conclusion

Including animals in your Spirit work will only aid in your understanding of this element. Unlike many other types of Spirit allies, with animals you might have the opportunity to physically see them in the world around you. Being able to see, smell, and touch a Spirit animal can help you to have a better understanding not only of that animal but also of yourself as a spiritual being. Animals are pure. They simply are what they are, without letting the influence of the talking self get in the way, like many of us humans do.

PART 3

RECIPES, RITUALS & SPELLCRAFT

"What art offers is space—
a certain breathing room for the spirit."

—JOHN UPDIKE

Chapter 9

INTUITION AND DIVINATION

Much of what Spirit offers to us is a connection to something beyond our own consciousness. It helps us listen to our own intuitive voice. Through the messages of Spirit, we can begin to discern what is our own intuition and what is fear or anxiety coming through. Having a solid relationship with our intuition helps us to use the tool of divination more successfully.

Divination is a form of Spirit communication. When Spirit wants to speak to us, it tends to use symbols and imagery. It doesn't typically speak with language. When we learn to translate the message of Spirit from images into language, we are stepping deeper into relationship with Spirit and with our intuitive voice. The two go hand in hand.

Intuition

One definition of intuition is the ability to understand something immediately without the conscious need to reason. When you start to trust and listen to your intuition, you are listening to the feeling part of yourself rather than the thinking part. Thinking and feeling are two different ways of processing information. One isn't better than the other, but they can each provide perspective.

When you approach a situation from a place of thinking, you open up to the potential for fear and anxiety getting in the way. When you approach a situation from a place of feeling, you bypass the fears that the thinking part of you might put in your way.

The thinking part of you makes decisions based on past information. This isn't a bad thing, but your thinking self might be running on an old program that hasn't been upgraded yet. And having awareness of all these things doesn't mean you suddenly become perfect. You will have backslides and times of doubt. You will revert to old negative patterns. This is part of being human. When you can catch yourself in these negative patterns and bring yourself back to a place of positive thoughts, you grow and improve.

The dominant culture doesn't really support people being in relationship with their intuition. People will say to "trust your gut," but what exactly does that mean and, more importantly, how do you do it?

Science is just starting to catch up to the idea that our guts and our brains communicate on levels that aren't speech-related.[71] The mind-gut connection is something that is being explored to help people with digestive issues and depression and/or anxiety. It is becoming clear that these things are related. The gut doesn't just send signals to the brain; they have two-way conversations.

Our gut instincts are literally wired into us as part of our survival instincts. The brain-gut connection can not only help us find that intuitive voice but also aid us in making decisions. This relationship is a direct link to our spirit and the energy of Spirit. We can see the element of Water in our blood. Fire can be found in our neurons and the electrical systems in the body. Our bones are

71 Johns Hopkins Medicine, "The Brain-Gut Connection."

of the element of Earth. The element of Air is in our every breath. We find Spirit in our gut feelings and intuition.

The voice of your gut may be an old familiar friend, but the truth of the matter is that the gut voice is like a muscle. The more you use it, the easier it becomes to use—or hear.

EXERCISE: Meeting Your Intuitive Self

For this trance exercise, you may need to have someone read the script to you or you can record it and play it back for yourself. It helps to perform this exercise when you have time and space after the trance to explore the feelings that came up for you.

Needs

At least thirty minutes of uninterrupted time

Journal and pen

Glass of water

The Journey

Take some deep breaths and allow yourself to settle in and relax. Breathe deeply and slowly. (*Pause here.*)

As you breathe, allow yourself to slowly sink into the space where you are sitting. With each breath, sink down further and further, as if gently pulled down below. As you breathe, your body softens, expands, and sinks into the earth below. Breathe gently and slowly, sinking down safe, secure, and calm.

As you begin to sink deeper into the earth, you feel yourself begin to move sideways. You feel yourself called to your sacred space. You travel along, moving closer and closer to your sacred space. (*Pause here.*)

You feel yourself begin to rise up out of the earth, and as you do, you see before you a building. This is the home of your intuitive self. As you fully come out of the earth, the home of your intuitive self becomes more and more clear and solid. When you are fully standing in front of the home of your intuition, take a moment to look at the details of this place.

What type of home is this? What is its size and shape? What do you feel, smell, or notice around the area of this space for the intuitive self? Spend some time taking in the details of this place (*Pause here.*)

When you feel ready, walk forward into the home of your intuitive self. Step into the building, and as you do, the form of your intuitive self takes shape. Your intuitive self may look human or animal or amorphous; your intuitive self can take on any shape. Allow it to shift into its form, and take in any other details of this place. (*Pause here.*)

When your intuitive self is fully formed in front of you, take some time to talk with your intuitive self and see what information it may have for you. (*Pause here.*)

Knowing that your time in this place is limited, take some time to ask any questions of your intuitive self that you desire to have answers for. (*Pause here.*)

When you feel ready, ask your intuitive self what sign or symbol you should look out for when it has a specific message for you. (*Pause here.*)

Take a moment to thank your intuitive self. Knowing that you can return here at any time, say anything else that needs to be said at this time. (*Pause here.*)

Say goodbye to your intuitive self and turn around, exiting the home of your intuitive self. Step outside the door, and as you do, feel yourself begin to sink back into the earth again. Breathe slowly and let yourself sink back down, down, down into the earth below you.

Once under the earth, you begin to move sideways, being pulled back toward your body. Allow your awareness to shift and feel yourself lifting back up from the ground into your physical body. Let yourself move up, up, up, and fill up your body. Notice your edges and breathe into them. Notice the bottoms of your feet and the top of your head. Take a moment to breathe into these places.

When you feel ready, slowly open your eyes and look around your space. Slowly drink the glass of water and write down anything important or interesting that you want to remember from this experience.

Know Thyself

One of the first steps in developing your intuitive muscle is what I refer to as one of the keys of Witchcraft. That key I call *Know Thyself.* In the ancient Greek world, written above the Oracle of Delphi were the words *Know Thyself.* Understanding who we are, how we work, and why we are the way we are is the work of our lifetime. This exploration won't ever end because we continue to unfold and grow.

However, you can begin to unpack the early lessons of your life. By looking back at your childhood and some of the programming you may have received from your culture growing up or from your family of origin, you can learn a lot about your motivation and why you are the way you are.

It is also through this exploration that you can make changes. If there is an old message from childhood that no longer serves, you can change that message or delete it altogether. However, until you begin the process of excavation, you are moving through the world with no direction.

As you learn to know yourself more and more, that intuitive voice, that gut instinct, will become clear. It is easier to communicate with your intuition when you aren't being led astray by old messages or voices that aren't even yours but are just old messages from your early life.

Mindfulness

A mindfulness practice can help you to work on your intuitive skills. Being mindful sounds so easy, but our talking self—the little voice that constantly seems to be directing our lives—can make it a challenge. Mindfulness is the practice of being in the present moment. Is it easy for you to be present without judging, directing, or trying to interpret what is going on, and simply just be?

A mindfulness practice involves intentionally putting yourself into a present state of mind and allowing yourself to just be. It doesn't include scrolling through your phone, watching television, reading a book, or driving a car, all of which are distractions and the opposite of being mindful.

Sometimes a mindfulness practice can look like a meditative practice, and the two do have a lot in common. However, with some meditative practices you have something to "do." Chanting, singing, playing music, and repeating a mantra are all ways to engage with meditation, but not with mindfulness.

Mindfulness is also about being present in the moment. For example, mindful eating is the practice of slowing down and paying attention to each step of your meal. Make space to take in the scent of your food. Slowly cut the food, paying attention to how it feels. Slowly eat the food, chewing with intention, so that you are truly connected with the process.

Mindfulness is a practice of allowing yourself to be and be present. Take five minutes today to just be. Find a time when you can be alone and uninterrupted for at least five minutes and just sit. See what happens.

We can get so caught up in the day-to-day running of our lives that we forget to be present in them. This is where mindfulness comes into play. In this space, your intuitive voice becomes clearer and easier to understand.

EXERCISE: Talk to Your Intuition

If you don't already have a relationship with your intuitive voice, now is the time to start. Read this exercise, set down this book, and start to practice.

Need

A quiet place where you can be uninterrupted for at least fifteen minutes or longer

Journal and pen

The Journey

Take a few breaths and notice where your awareness currently resides. For many of us, our awareness is likely scattered. It might feel like it is "in our head," where our talking self resides. It might also be thinking about the cat litter, and work tomorrow, and what to make for dinner, and what our boss is thinking, and getting into that program, and, and, and.

Let yourself connect with all those threads of attention and reel them back into yourself. Sometimes I imagine little fishing lines that are my threads of awareness. I simply unhook those lines from where they are and reel them back into my body.

As you gather up all these threads of awareness, direct them to the top of your head. Reel in all these threads of awareness and pull up all the threads of awareness that are in your body until they form a glowing ball in the top of your head. Once these threads are all gathered there, pull that ball of awareness down your body.

Let that ball of awareness drop from the top of your head down behind your eyes and through your palate. Let your awareness continue to lower into your throat and neck, moving down your body. When that ball of glowing awareness reaches your heart, notice how it glows and activates the energy center that resides there.

The ball of awareness continues to sink lower and lower in your body until it comes to rest in your center, the place where you feel your gut is most active. When your ball of awareness reaches this place, allow it to unfurl a bit, opening and widening and being active in your gut.

If you notice that it is hard to keep your awareness in your gut, just be patient with the process and gather up those threads and send them back to your gut.

While your awareness is in this place, open and expansive, feel how your awareness and your gut interact. Is this easy and comfortable? Is it awkward? Is it a challenge? Just notice what comes up for you.

From this place, see if you can enter into a conversation with your gut, or your intuitive body. What does your intuitive voice have to say? How does it relate to your awareness and thinking body? Sit in this place of connection for as long as you can.

When you feel ready, allow that ball of glowing awareness to rise back up your body. As it does, the threads of awareness that want to go other places easily do. Allow your awareness to open up and return to its normal state of being. Allow that glowing ball to expand and release, returning to its more open and expansive state.

Write down anything important or interesting that came up during your conversation. At any time moving forward, you can connect in with your gut by sinking your awareness down into that part of your body.

Divination

Divination is the practice of using occult-connected techniques to gain hidden information or details of future events. It is using our skills as an embodied human to tap into the realm of Spirit. I would go out on a limb and say that what most modern divinatory practitioners are doing isn't what you might visualize a "fortune teller" doing. Although historically there have been fortune tellers who used their psychic gifts and skills to help people, that term has pretty much been relegated to mean fraud.

You don't have to have psychic abilities to use divination. I do believe that we all have psychic abilities and it is a muscle that can be strengthened. But I also believe that some folks come into this life with stronger abilities, or they experience something in this life that gives them a stronger starting-off point. However, using the tool of divination doesn't have to even touch on a psychic skill.

Divination is a tool for the intuition. The different forms of divination can help us explain what is coming through in our own intuitive messaging.

Psychic abilities and intuition are closely related, but they aren't the same thing. All of us are born with intuition; it is a human capacity that exists without any practice or prompting. We might learn to ignore it, but it is still present. Our intuition is about ourselves as individuals and how we relate to outside forces and experiences. Psychic ability, on the other hand, is often about information outside of ourselves or about other people. This isn't necessarily an inherent skill, but is one that can be developed with practice.

We are all born intuitive, but we aren't all born psychic.

With that in mind, not all forms of divination are created equal either! Some systems of divination require years of study to master. Some of them are made up of complex symbols that you need to be trained in to understand and correctly interpret. Some forms of divination might come easily to you, like you've known the symbols all your life, while others might always feel like a foreign language.

As a professional tarot reader, my experience has been that most clients are seeking confirmation on what they already feel to be true and/or they are feeling stuck and are uncertain about what steps to take next. Rarely do I get clients who want me to "tell their future." Then again, I work out of a spiritual shop where people are seeking spiritual work. If I was reading tarot cards at a county fair, my client base could be quite different.

The future isn't set in stone, and by seeking out the skill of divination, you hold a key to change the future. If anyone attempts to sell you on the idea that they can totally predict the future and will give you a 100 percent guarantee, they are not to be trusted. Don't give them your money!

Types of Divination

There are hundreds of types of divination practices, everything from astrology to tarot cards to reading the entrails of sacrificed animals. However, the following list includes the styles of divination that are more common, popular, and accessible to most of us.

Astrology

Astrology is the study of the relationship of the stars and celestial bodies and their patterns and movements in the sky to our lives. Each person is born with their own astrological chart that shows what the sky was up to at the time they were born. As the planets and celestial bodies move through the sky, their movements correspond to events in the person's life. An astrologer can look at these upcoming patterns and help you divine what is going to happen in the coming time frame.

Automatic Writing

Automatic writing is the process of going into a meditative state and allowing a spirit to move through the body, using the individual's hands to write messages. During this process, the practitioner opens up to Spirit, clears their mind, and allows their hand to simply move while holding a pen against paper. Without trying to think or force the writing, the practitioner simply allows the words to flow.

Bibliomancy

Bibliomancy is the process of flipping through a book and allowing your intuition to determine when to stop and land on a sentence. That sentence then offers a glimpse into what you need to know. This process can be a little like going to visit the Oracle of Delphi, because the answer doesn't always make sense. It can come through as a more poetic answer than clear, directional information.

Candle Reading

Candle reading can happen in several ways. While a candle is burning, you can use the flame to divine, looking for signs and symbols in the flickering of the flame. This is referred to as scrying (rhymes with "crying"). As the candle melts, you can read the melted wax, looking for any signs or symbols in the drips. If you are burning a candle in a container, you can read the soot and wax that might be left on the sides of the container.

Cowrie Shells

Using cowrie shells as a form of divination comes from Africa and the African diaspora. This form of divination is done using only four cowrie shells. A question is asked and the shells are tossed on the reading surface. How they land, up or down and in what form and pattern, determines the answer to the question. There are sixteen possible outcomes.

Dice

Using dice for divination is an ancient practice that can be found in most cultures around the world. In some systems, bones or stones are used with specific carvings (usually numbers) on each side or flat surface. But regular numbered dice are also very common. The numbers all correspond to an answer or outcome.

I Ching

The I Ching is a Chinese form of divination that translates into English as the *Book of Changes*. In this practice, there are stalks of yarrow tossed down to create a pattern of numbers. There are sixty-four possible outcomes, depending on how the staves lay out. These numbers are then read in the book of *I Ching*. Often the answers come through as poetic, leaving a lot of room for interpretation.

Ogham

The Ogham (pronounced "OM") alphabet comes from the Celtic peoples. The letters are small horizontal line markings set off a central vertical line that connects to certain kinds of sacred trees from the land. Each of these trees holds a deeper meaning and is also a form of the alphabet.

Oracle Cards

Oracle cards are a type of divination using artwork on a card. There are thousands of different oracle decks on the market, and each one has its own unique set of symbols and meanings. Learning one type of oracle deck will not translate to another. Each one will have its own special system based on the artwork and the author.

Palmistry

Palmistry is the reading of the lines, mounds, and shapes of the palms of the hands and fingers. Each line, finger, and segment is connected to a planet or energy. The shape of the lines, the length, and the thickness all have meaning and can give information about life paths.

Pendulums

Pendulums are stones or other charms that hang from a chain or string. They are held in the dominant hand, and the movement of the swinging of that charm gives the answer. Pendulums are typically used for yes-no questions, but they have also been used to diagnose illness, determine the gender of babies, and correct imbalances in the body. There are also pendulum mats that can be made or purchased that work much like a Ouija board, with the pendulum swinging over the answer.

Runes

Although there are a few different styles of runes, they all originated in the Germanic and Nordic cultures. The runes are an alphabet, with each letter holding a specific correspondence and meaning. In myths, the runes were discovered by the god Odin. Each letter has a spiritual correspondence. For a reading, you either toss out the runes or pick a few at random. The meaning of the symbols gives you the information you seek.

Scrying

Scrying is a visualization practice. Ultimately it is the process of allowing your eyes to soften and allow your psychic senses to grow while you gaze at an object, looking for signs and symbols. The object you gaze upon could be a crystal, a flame or fire, a bowl of water, water with ink in it or ice melting, a cracked egg in a bowl of water, or any other number of things. The point of scrying is to find signs and symbols through the object being gazed upon.

Signs and Omens

Signs and omens are wide and varied. You divine messages through the seemingly random interactions you have with the world around you. You may divine messages through an encounter with a wild animal or by watching how birds fly, reading the shapes of clouds in the sky, watching thunderstorms, and so forth. Signs and omens are often connected to cultural superstitions, like rain on a wedding day.

Tarot

Tarot is a specific system that is based on an ancient card game. Many countries claim to have created the tarot game, but it is unclear where the system officially started. The modern tarot is typically based on the Rider-Waite-Smith system, which has its roots in the Golden Dawn fraternal order from the late 1800s and early 1900s. In most modern decks, there are seventy-eight cards, and each has its own meanings. Reading the cards involves looking at the message of each individual card as well as the message in the overall layout of the cards.

Tea Leaf/Coffee Ground Reading

Tea leaf and coffee ground readings are found in many cultures all over the world. The concept is to drink the tea or coffee and then, when finished, ritually swirl and turn the cup over into a saucer. The leftover herbs or grounds leave patterns or signs in the cup, and this is what is read to gain information.

Throwing Bones and Curios

Throwing bones is just what it sounds like: tossing some bones on a layout and interpreting how they land and what the meaning might be. In modern bone throwing, readers also have *curios*, or personal objects, in their collection of bones. These have specific meanings that only that reader knows. It is a highly personal way to divine.

Divination Preparation

Before performing a reading or using your favorite form of divination, it's a good idea to give yourself a moment to step into the right mind space. Before you even pick up your divination tool, take a few deep breaths. Give yourself a moment to come into mindfulness, being fully present in the moment. It can help to do a little scan of your body and spirit to see if there is anything that needs adjustment or shifting.

As you breathe, take a moment connect with your Witch's eye, sometimes referred to as the third eye. This is the spot just above and between your normal seeing eyes. It is believed that this is our spiritual center of foresight. Send some breath into this spot.

When you feel ready, use an intuitive anointing oil to anoint this spot on your head and help you further open your Witch's eye and connect with your intuition.

Divination Oil

This recipe is based on the formula we use at my shop, Milk & Honey. Use this oil to help activate your intuitive self before performing divination or any time you want to engage with your intuition.

This recipe is for a half-ounce oil bottle with a solid lid or cap. In the bottom of the bottle, put a small quartz crystal and a dried jasmine blossom. Then add the essential oils listed here. Finally, add your base oil to fill the rest of the bottle. Grapeseed or almond oil is best.

A small quartz crystal
A dried jasmine blossom
5 drops thyme essential oil
5 drops rose essential oil
3 drops cinnamon essential oil
3 drops bay leaf essential oil
½ ounce base oil

Conclusion

Intuition and divination are closely connected. We need to have a solid relationship with our intuition in order to be successful at divination. Both of these things are part of our Spirit. We all have the capacity to be intuitive because it is an inherent part of our spiritual nature.

Chapter 10

DRAWING DOWN AND ASPECTING

The Oracle of Delphi in Greece is still one of the world's most well-known centers of prophecy. In the ancient world, this site was known for the priestesses who performed and provided oracles to the people who sought out their wisdom. Apparently, this site was originally the location of a Dionysian cult and later became a temple to Apollo. The priestess at Delphi was called the Pythia; it was believed that she was channeling the voice of the Goddess to those seeking wisdom.

There is some evidence that the caves where these priestesses did their work had fissures in the walls that allowed for hallucinogenic steam to come through. This may be how these oracles received their visions. The words they spoke were often in riddles, so it was difficult to discern what the messages actually meant. Although there is some evidence of this hallucinogenic influence, it isn't considered a historical fact.

The Norse practice of Seidr is a trance technique where the Seidkona, or prophetess, goes into a trance state. In this state, she is able to speak with beings in the other realms. She can call upon the dead, the gods, and any other spiritual being to seek answers to the questions being asked. The modern term for this practice is referred to as spaework or oracular seidh (or seidr). At one time there were Seidkona who traveled from village to village offering their gift of sight for payment.

In the African diaspora, especially in Voudon, Umbanda, and Santeria, there is a practice of being trance-possessed by the gods; this process is often referred to as "being ridden." The individual whom the gods choose is called the "horse." Most often the individual who has ritually prepared in advance to be ridden is the one whom the spirits choose, but this isn't always the case. Occasionally someone who just came to watch the ritual will be chosen by the gods.

There are even some Christian traditions where people go into a deep trance through prayer and get possessed by the Holy Spirit. Once possessed by the spirit of God, these practitioners will begin to speak in tongues, offer prophecy, or perform hands-on healings.

Modern Possession

In many modern Witchcraft traditions, we also see practices of trance possession, or what is often called *drawing down*. The term *drawing down the moon* originated in Wiccan circles. However, there are several traditions where the high priestess would "draw down the moon" during ritual. In this part of the ritual, the high priest calls the Goddess into the body of the high priestess. When the high priestess calls the God into the high priest, this is referred to as *drawing down the sun*.

This is a very gendered way of looking at trance possession. In the early days of these traditions, women were the only ritualists who "drew down" female deities and men only did this type of ritual work with male deities. But this is really no longer the case. And this idea of the moon being feminine and the sun being masculine has rather fallen by the wayside. Our magical practices are moving beyond the confines of gender, for truly, the gods are beyond the confines of gender. More and more, I see the term *drawing down* being used for the overall practice.

Inspiration

The lightest form of drawing down, or aspecting, is what I refer to as *inspiration*. This was taught to me during my training in the Reclaiming Tradition of Witchcraft. With the practice of inspiration, we call the gods into our circle and ask for their influence, but we don't call them into our bodies.

With inspiration, we might hear a deity whisper in our ear or feel their hands on our shoulders. Through this process, we may find ourselves inspired to try something new or get a spark of an idea.

One of the exercises we often use in the Reclaiming Tradition as a way to start practicing these skills is what is called "pass the cloak aspecting." With this technique, the deity is called into a cloak or veil. During the ritual, we invite them to inhabit the fabric and lend their energy to anyone who should wear this piece of clothing.

The veil or cloak is then passed around to the ritual participants so that everyone gets an opportunity to "wear the Goddess" or feel the influence of their deity's energy on their body. Again, this is an influential energy, but it isn't possession in any way. These practices help us open to the voice and energy of an entity that isn't ourselves. Plus, it is a safe magical practice, keeping a strong boundary between the practitioner and the deity.

Aspecting

The next level of possession in Witchcraft circles is what I think of as *aspecting* but many traditions might still call *drawing down*. This is the practice of inviting the deity to share your body. Although this is not a full trance possession, many ritualists who utilize this technique often have very little to no recollection of what took place while they were in aspect.

Aspecting is considered an advanced magical technique and should not be taken on lightly. It is important that the practitioner have a strong grounding practice and experience with some level of shadow work.

After an aspecting encounter with a deity, the practitioner will forever be changed. It is like taking a peek into someone else's life. You can't just turn back to how things were before that moment. Not all deities have happy stories or energies. When you invite these beings into your body, you take on some of that energy potentially forever.

Typically with aspecting, it is best if there is a previous relationship with the deity being drawn down. Aspecting tends to go more smoothly when the ritualist and the deity are already familiar with each other. The ritualist and the deity need to communicate before the ritual begins. Boundaries need to be set before stepping into ritual space. This is why having a solid relationship is helpful. Think about being intimate with a stranger versus someone you know well.

Before Drawing Down

Before the actual process of aspecting, or drawing down, happens, the practitioner and the deity should make some agreements. The boundaries and agreements that are set beforehand could be simple things, like you only give permission for the deity to speak with your voice but not control your legs or where you walk, or it could be that you ask the deity not to run around the ritual space. One of the challenges with aspecting is that deities don't fully understand how delicate human bodies are and they might want to try something that your body can't do. It is important to make this clear before calling them in.

Even if the ritualist doesn't remember anything from the aspecting process, part of them is always present. There is a human filter that never goes away. There is no excuse for bad behavior from a ritualist when they are in aspect. The excuse "the Goddess made me do it" isn't an acceptable one. If there is a ritualist who continually uses the tool of aspecting as a way to say cruel or negative things or manipulate the ritual, then they aren't really ready to use this advanced ritual technique.

Trance Possession

Full trance possession is a deeper release of control on the part of the ritualist. Full trance possession is fully allowing your consciousness to go somewhere else and letting deity fully take over your body. This is a very advanced technique and is something that most modern Western occult practitioners aren't really trained to do.

Full trance possession isn't something you can learn in a weekend workshop or from watching videos online. This is a profound and intense experience that requires deep trance and ritual techniques to allow for altered states, and it takes time. Many modern Witchcraft rituals are about ninety minutes long. For a full trance possession, it can take hours or even days for the ritual to get participants into the right state.

In traditions that use full trace possession, there are specific symbols, chants, and drum rhythms that are used to help the possession process. Specific entities are drawn to their symbols. Many ritualists train for years before ever being ready to fully be possessed.

Aspecting Preparation

No matter what level of drawing down is being attempted, some preparation work is necessary. The first step, of course, is to understand the entity being invoked. Is this a being you know well and have a strong relationship with? If not, you should start studying and performing rituals to learn more about them.

Many ritualists going into drawing down will partake in a short fast and spend time in meditation before the ritual. It can be helpful to spend some time praying to the deity or making offerings to that entity as a way to connect before the ritual starts.

Some ritualists also perform mind-altering techniques to help shift their consciousness and more easily step into an altered state. There are many ways to shift consciousness, and not all of them are ideal for a ritual situation. What works for you as a ritualist might not work as well for someone else, so keep that in mind as well. Mind-altering techniques are things like breathwork, fasting, meditation cues, and even taking mind-altering substances.

In my training with Reclaiming, I learned a process that works really well for me. Before inviting the deity's energy into my body, I take some time to slowly and intentionally drop my consciousness down. I do a visualization process where I allow my awareness to slowly flow down my body. I gather my awareness into a ball of energy right below my feet. This ball of consciousness will go anywhere I go. It is safe and protected and can easily snap back into my body if needed.

During the aspecting process, if I notice my consciousness trying to take control, I just pause and send that awareness back into the ball at my feet. It's like emptying the vessel so the deity can fill it up.

A lot of shifting awareness is tricking the consciousness into letting go of control. Here are some other ways to approach that.

Chanting, Singing, Drumming

Repetitive chanting, singing, and drumming can help us step into altered states. Hearing repetitive rhythms, especially if they hold specific beats, can shift our brain patterns and allow us to move into different states of consciousness.

Hallucinogenic Substances

There are plenty of substances that can alter the mind and the spirit. These aren't required in order to shift states of consciousness and they should never be ingested without the clear intention of stepping into a magical state. Plus, in many areas hallucinogenic substances are illegal.

Visualization

Having a clear visualization process can help you move from a mundane state of mind into a magical one. There are tons of different visualizations that can work for aspecting. It's all about finding the right one for you.

Deprivation

It's scientifically proven that a lack of food and sleep shifts our brain patterns. By intentionally going into a state of deprivation, some find it easier to draw down. Of course, this is ideal for a healthy body. And if you have any health issues, such as diabetes, sleep disorders, and the like, this should not be practiced.

Hypnotic Induction

The literal drawing down process can work as a hypnotic induction. Words are triggers and can be carefully used to enter into a hypnotic state. In that place, it is much easier to shift your consciousness aside and allow Spirit to enter your body.

Dancing

Continuous dancing and movement is another form of deprivation, but it can also alter consciousness on its own. Have you ever been on a dance floor and just let yourself go? That's how dancing can help shift awareness; as you get tired, you enter into a state of deprivation.

Masking or Veiling

By putting on a mask or a veil, you literally change your view of the world. This altered state of awareness can also shift your consciousness. Over time, if you work with this practice, it can also become a trigger to help you shift into an altered state just by putting the mask or veil on.

Scourging or Ligature

Self-flagellation and being bound are both forms of deprivation. When done in a ritual space, they can help to shift consciousness.

Breathwork

Different forms of breathing can literally shift your awareness. Holotropic breathing, for example, can put you in a state of hyperventilation, which is another form of deprivation and will shift your consciousness.

During ritual, it's best if there is a formal acknowledgment that drawing down is happening. This is most often done with a spoken-word invocation. A ritualist, or *tender*, will help the practitioner get into the right space and call that deity into their body. Often the words "speak with their mouth, see with their eyes, move with their body," or other such things are said to help the deity to come through and the practitioner's consciousness to take a back seat.

Tenders

In Reclaiming, we always have a *tender* for anyone taking on the role of aspecting. This is the ritualist who watches over the practitioner in aspect, makes sure they have what they need, and helps them to interact with the other ritual participants, if such a thing is required. The tender will also help the practitioner go into aspect and come back into their body once that part of the ritual is complete.

Often tenders will also keep track of anything important or interesting that the deity might have said. The person in aspect isn't always capable of remembering what comes through, and the tender becomes a ritual watcher to gain these nuggets of wisdom.

Depending on the size of the ritual, the deity may want to speak to the entire group or interact with specific people. These are all things that should be discussed before the ritual begins.

Before opening up sacred space and performing ritual devocations, the deity invited into the practitioner should be released and sent back to their lovely realms. For some, the process of letting go of an entity is easy; their consciousness slides back into its space. For others, or at other times, it is more challenging to let go. This is another place where it is important to have a solid tender to assist.

• • • •

Fire and Spirit

Josephine Winter is the author of *Fire Magic* and *Witchcraft Discovered*. For over two decades she has traded the ordinary for the arcane, weaving Norse Heathenry into Alexandrian Wicca and now leading a coven. Her magical background, along with degrees in education, literature, and the arts, fuel her approach to teaching and co-founding Lepus Lumen, a grassroots collective of covens and individuals who deliver free courses to Witches in several different locations around Australia. Josie lives with her family and lots of books in Australia's leafy southeast.

I BURNED MY first actual effigy when I was twenty-five.

I'm sure there were other, similar experiences before that—big bonfires that lit up entire hillsides in the countryside where I grew up, or dressing roadside stumps in human clothing because they appeared a bit person-shaped when you looked at them just so. But it wasn't until I was grown that I camped in remote bushland with fifty strangers and built a man two storeys high from sticks and branches with the express intention of setting him alight and destroying him.

His insides were an iron skeleton that clicked together and to which we tied our bundles of sticks. We spent a whole day constructing him, chatting and bonding with each other as we worked. I made friends there that I still have today. As the sun set, we stood in a circle around the man and a ritual was performed, with torches and chanting and drumming. A mirror was passed around to the participants and we each saw ourselves: *only* ourselves, and the man looming behind us. He stood and stared at our reflections sullenly over our shoulders, representing that which we would leave behind on that frosty Samhain night in the bush: our fears, our reservations, our worries, our grief, our inaction.

Once we could look ourselves in the eye and the drumbeat slowed to a sonorous pulse, we set him alight. The flames licked timidly at first but soon took hold and grew into a roaring inferno, sending sparks swirling fifty metres or more up into the night sky, where they mingled with the stars themselves.

I set the fire. I chanted and danced and whooped in elation. That night I knew what I needed to do.

The element of fire, with its associations of courage, passion, transformation, creativity, and more, is the first of the four that comes to mind when I think of spirit. One's spirit can be aflame with passion, lust, inspiration, or even rage. We talk of bad news or events dampening the spirit, as if it is a physical fire. High spirits are present when a group of people are in a good mood but dwindle into low spirits during periods of difficulty or stagnation.

That night in the bush, as I danced with people who had been strangers to me a week earlier and watched the people around the fire glowing from within and without after a ritual experience, what was kindled in me was a love of community and of sharing my magical and spiritual practice with other like-minded souls. Up until that point, I had been for the most part a consumer of group ritual and communal experience: I turned up, I took part, I had fun, I went home.

But that taste of the infinite—the little whiff of divinity I experienced that night—inspired me to seek it out more, to honour it as I was able to. My spiritual fires had been well and truly stoked, and my life changed immensely from that moment. That night was the catalyst I needed to step up and offer to organise or run ritual for the group I was a part of at the time. I formed community groups and volunteered at events. In time, it would give me the courage to seek out Traditional Wicca and eventually find the magical family I had yearned for over many years.

When that first ever effigy burned down and the fire sat as a bonfire atop a huge pile of embers, the looming iron skeleton remained, glowing orange and then a deep blood red against the backdrop of the dark forest. Red slowly faded to black, and by the morning the structure was cool enough to touch in the slim autumn sunlight. The fire had burned down to almost nothing, as fires do.

My newfound passion for community building and group lasted much longer than that, but it, too, waned. For several years, every weekend and some weeknights, too, were chock-full of community events, rituals, coffee meetups, pub gatherings, workshops, committee meetings, conferences and more. These were often quite far away, and my full-time job funded these trips and ate up the rest of my life. Initially this didn't bother me, but after a few years, well… sometimes we're so busy being aflame with passion for something that we don't realise that flame is burning through us like so many bundles of sticks.

I got tired. Then I got jaded. Then I was thoroughly burned through. Social gatherings started to feel stale to me. Meetings that used to feel inspiring and fizzing with creative energy now felt like herding kittens. Organising and running group ritual changed too—so slowly that I didn't notice until it was too late—from an act of shared communion with the Divine to an onerous slog of churning out and enacting material that only made me feel stressed out. My inner flame was all but extinguished, and I didn't know why.

In time, I put down all my community work and fell into a bit of a slump. I wallowed in my burnout black hole and felt like a failure, and spent a long time not doing much more than this. It wasn't until I started examining these feelings and what had led to them in a more reflective way, and one that took into account the spiritual experience I'd had all those years ago—that spark of creativity, the burning fire of my passion for the work, the warmth of connection, and the transformative nature of group ritual done well and regularly—that I realised this was an inner issue and one that could be understood through the lenses of elemental fire and spirit.

If a fire is left to burn too intensely for too long without enough fuel or oxygen, the flames eventually dwindle, leaving behind only ashes and smoke. The initial intensity that might have been productive turns destructive. In Western magic and esotericism, the dynamic, active spirit of fire can become destructive if uncontrolled, leading to chaos, anger, and aggression. My work in community had burned so hot for so long that I had turned in on myself, and as I tired or tried to force things, chaos ensued.

Rather than trying to push through when I started to waver in this work, I would have done well to remember that all fire needs fuel, and a fire with a solid bed of coals will burn quietly all night. At the height of energy and inspiration, I could have banked that energy and worked in a more sustainable way, taking breaks for as long as I needed to, with confidence in the knowledge that what I had built would probably still be there if I turned away for a while, and if it wasn't ... well, then it wasn't.

No fire burns forever, and one of the lessons of fire and spirit is that even the best times don't go on forever. At the peak of my community-building era, I wasn't willing to see this, and that fact made me blind to things failing until it was too late. It would have been more beneficial for all concerned if I had accepted that everything has a season, rather than try to run bigger and more unwieldy groups and events for longer and longer.

Fire, too, teaches us about creativity and destruction. It is the only element that can be created or destroyed (think lighting a fire or snuffing out a candle). When our hearts and minds no longer "catch fire" with inspiration, we can no longer create in a meaningful way. Feeling tired and jaded and pushing on anyway not only made my outer community work no longer bring me joy but also affected my own personal work and how I approached my craft. Suddenly many of my most deeply held beliefs and practices started to feel like drudgery.

Like a fire that roars with initial intensity but eventually consumes its fuel, our passions, if left untended and unchecked, can lead to burnout. The vibrant flame that once ignited connection and creativity can dwindle to mere embers, leaving behind a sense of exhaustion and disillusionment. However, just as a fire can be rekindled with care and the right nourishment, so too can our inner spirit be reignited through reflection, rest, and a renewed understanding of the cyclical nature of energy.

In the end, the journey with the element of fire, both literally on that transformative Samhain night in the bush and metaphorically in the fervent dedication to community that I held for many years and still hold today (albeit in more manageable amounts), reveals a crucial lesson about the nature of spirit and energy. For me, the experience serves as a potent reminder that sustainable engagement, mindful of the need for both intense burning and quiet tending, is essential to keep the fires of our passions alight without being consumed by them.

Ultimately, recognising the finite nature of even the most fervent flames allows us to appreciate their warmth and light while learning to step back and allow for the natural ebb and flow of energy, ensuring that the potential for creative and communal fire can be sparked anew when the time is right.

Josephine Winter

• • • •

Post-Aspecting Side Effects

Even the most positive aspecting experience can have some side effects. There are things to look out for after the deity has been dismissed. Having several of these issues after a ritual can lead to a ritual hangover.

A ritual hangover can feel a lot like an alcohol hangover. It could happen right after the ritual, a few hours later, or even the next day. A ritual hangover can manifest as a headache, feeling nauseous, feeling out of sorts, or even feeling cranky or unusually emotional. Some of the physical reactions that can come up right after aspecting might be signs that a hangover is headed your way, but if you ground, drink some water, have something to eat, and, if all else fails, take a shower or bath, you can avoid it. Here are some things to look out for.

Dizziness

It's not unusual to feel dizzy after having massive amounts of energy moving through your body. This is a sign that grounding is needed. Food and water are a close second.

Shaking

When big energy suddenly leaves your body, it can feel a little bit like going into shock. Shaking is one of the signs of big energy depletion. Food and water will help.

Dissociation

Letting go of the magic can be a challenge. If it feels like you can't let go or the deity won't let go, or if it feels like this world isn't real, that's a clear sign of dissociation. Getting into a cold shower can help. Getting hydrated and having a good sleep can also help.

Body Temperature Drop

During the process of aspecting, you are running a lot of energy through your body. When you release the entity from your body, it can cause a rapid drop in body temperature. Simply putting on a sweater or blanket can solve this problem. It is important to remember that this is a temporary issue.

Collapse

When deity first leaves your body, it can feel like a wave of energy leaving you. On rare occasions this may cause you to feel like your body can't stay upright. Often this feels like you need to sit down, or you sink down as soon as the deity has left. Food and drink can help shift this.

Euphoria

Aspecting, or drawing down, is a joyful experience. It is mind-altering. When you return to full consciousness, you might have feelings of euphoria. You may feel like laughing or crying. Emotions may run high afterward. Talking about your experience, grounding, and getting into a bath or shower can help with this.

Returning to the Body

Occasionally a ritualist might have a hard time fully returning to their body. There are some tricks for the tender to use to help them be fully back in their body.

Ask Mundane Questions

When you ask someone to focus on things from their mundane life, it helps to shift their consciousness back into the driver's seat. Mundane questions are things like, What is on the back of your toilet seat? What is your address or phone number? What is the name of your boss? What kind of car do you drive?

Food and Water

A lot of grounding challenges can be solved by drinking water and eating food. These are both normal grounding practices and are easy to use.

Salt Under the Tongue

This is an old-school grounding technique. Salt under the tongue goes into the bloodstream faster and helps a person sink deeper into their physical body.

Water

Sometimes if you threaten the ritualist with tossing them in a river, cold pool, or cold shower, the threat is shocking enough to shake them back to reality. And if the threat doesn't work, literally put them in cold water.

Conclusion

Before you go down the road of aspecting, trance possession, or drawing down, it is important to ask yourself why you want to do this. Does it seem like a cool parlor trick? Do you like the idea of having ritual participants bow down to you as an emanation of the Goddess? Do you want to feed your ego?

Be honest.

It's not unusual to desire to have the skill of trance possession, but it is important that you know your truth before taking on this advanced technique. When aspecting at a larger ritual, people will bow down to you. People will share secrets with you. People will be awed by your presence. This is extremely humbling and occasionally awkward. Sometimes people will view you differently after the ritual, always seeing that deity connected to you.

A ritualist holding the energy of a deity is not the one being honored in ritual; the deity is being honored. Having that clear and separate in your mind and spirit is essential for having a healthy practice. I've seen many a Witch get a big ego after holding a deity in a big public ritual and feeling shiny and special for the role. Yes, it is special, but it doesn't make the ritualist a god, only a servant to the magic.

If you want to learn these techniques in order to deepen your relationship with a deity, then you are on the right track. If you want to learn these techniques because you want to expand your skills as a ritualist, then you are on the right track. If you want to learn this process to better serve your community, then you are on the right track.

Chapter 11

SPIRIT SPELLS, RECIPES, AND RITUALS

Much of the magic of Spirit is connected to practices of self-improvement, increasing consciousness, and stepping more fully into ourselves as magical practitioners. Spells and rituals for Spirit are connected to our higher chakra energy centers, helping us to step more deeply into the magical and mystical world.

The following spells, recipes, and rituals can be used at any time and any place. They are meant to help you work on your relationship with Spirit based on the specific nuance of each ritual. Some of these rituals may include a trance or meditation. It's good to pre-record these and listen to them during the actual ritual.

Some of these rituals also include recipes for ritual ingredients or food to make for after the ritual completion.

General Blessing Ritual

We often forget to take care of ourselves magically. This is a ritual to help you slow down and direct some of your magical power right back to you! Before starting, read through the entire ritual and prepare the special Bless Your Cheese Buns and the Blessing Oil. Both recipes follow the ritual instructions.

Needs

Candles for light

Large bowl of water

1 large flower

A mirror (preferably full-length)

Blessing Oil (recipe follows)

Bless Your Cheese Buns (recipe follows)

Journal and pen

Directions

Before the ritual, allow yourself the time and space to take a long cleansing bath or shower. Really take your time with this process, clearing off any energy that you don't need to be carrying. Cleanse your physical and your spiritual body.

When you are finished with the bath, dry off and stay naked or wear clothes that are loose, flowing, and comfortable.

In your ritual space, light all the candles and turn off any electric lights. Place the bowl of water and the large flower in the center of your space. Place the mirror near the bowl of water. Have the Blessing Oil close at hand. Add anything else that you feel called to include in your ritual space.

When you feel ready, stand in front of the mirror. If you are wearing clothes, consider taking them off for this process. Pick up the Blessing Oil and begin to ritually anoint yourself. Take your time with this process. Remember that each time you anoint yourself, you are giving yourself a blessing.

Place oil on the following parts of your body:

- Feet
- Sex
- Low belly

- Navel
- Heart
- Throat
- Palms
- Third eye
- Top of the head

When you are finished with all the anointing, bow to yourself in the mirror. Look at yourself and speak out loud the blessings that you are offering. Let yourself speak from the heart and bless yourself for your bravery.

When you feel ready, sit down in front of the mirror with the bowl of water. If you want to put your clothes back on, now would be the time, but you can also stay naked if that feels comfortable for you. Place the flower in the bowl of water.

Allow your eyes to soften as you watch the flower float along in the bowl of water. See if you can scry into the water. Pay attention to any signs, symbols, letters, or numbers that seem to show up in the bowl of water. Also pay attention to your intuitive voice and see if any messages want to come through that voice. Allow this process to slowly unfold, even if it feels a little awkward or uncomfortable. Keep at it for some time.

When it feels complete, anoint yourself with the water. Open up your ritual space and write down anything important or interesting that came up. If you'd like, you can pour the water into a jar to save it for anointing your third eye.

Enjoy your homemade Bless Your Cheese Buns.

Blessing Oil

This recipe is based on the Blessing Oil that we make at my shop, Milk & Honey. You will need essential oils and a base oil of almond or grapeseed to put the essential oils into. This recipe makes ½ ounce of magical oil.

Ingredients

5 drops cedar essential oil

5 drops sweet orange essential oil

2 drops neroli essential oil

½ ounce base oil

Bless Your Cheese Buns

Make these cheese buns to enjoy after your blessing ritual. They are delicious and will help you ground.

Ingredients

1 tablespoon yeast

¼ cup hot water

⅓ cup milk

½ cup vegetable oil

1 teaspoon salt

3 cups all-purpose flour

8 ounces cheddar cheese, chopped into small bits

1 egg white, beaten

Directions

In a small bowl, combine the yeast and water and set aside. In a large bowl, combine the milk, oil, and salt. Add the yeast mixture to the milk and then slowly add in the flour one cup at a time. This should start to form a dough. Turn the dough out onto a floured surface and knead for 10 minutes.

Divide the dough into twelve even balls and press the balls flat. Put some cheese in the center of each flattened ball and then fold the dough around the cheese. Set the balls of dough to rise until they have doubled in size, about 45 minutes.

Preheat the oven to 375 degrees F. Brush the tops of the balls with egg white and bake for 15 minutes until golden brown.

Transformation Ritual

If you are feeling stuck and ready for a change, this is an excellent ritual to perform. It can help open you up to the possibility of transformation and make room for changes to come through. This ritual can be performed at any time, but if possible consider it for a new moon. Before the ritual, create the blessed water and the transformation elixir. The recipes follow the ritual instructions.

Needs

- Slips of paper and a pen
- Cauldron or large pot
- Lighter or matches
- 3 pinches of blessed or kosher salt
- Blessed water (recipe follows)
- Object to represent transformation (stone, jewelry, altar item)
- Transformational Cassis Elixir (recipe follows)
- Journal and pen

Directions

Create an altar with all the objects listed above. This ritual calls for an object of transformation. This can be any object that you feel represents the change you desire. Ideally this would be something small that can be worn or easily carried with you.

Take a moment to ground and center yourself. Breathe and notice if you have any energy shooting off in directions other than the present moment. Call all those pieces of yourself back to your body.

Take a moment to acknowledge that you are stepping into ritual space. You may want to draw an energetic barrier around your ritual space. Call in any spiritual allies you want to help you with this working. When you feel ready, take some time to sit in meditation. Allow your thoughts to go toward where you are feeling stuck or ready for a change.

Perhaps you have a clear and distinct answer to where the blockages or obstacles are, or perhaps not. Just allow yourself to be open to the potential for change and transformation. If you feel so called, speak out loud to your guides and allies, letting them know you are ready for a change. Write down anything important or interesting that comes through while in this contemplative space.

If you find a specific place where change needs to happen or a specific situation that is causing an obstacle, write that down on one of the slips of paper. Write down any specific places where you are feeling stuck. These could be major or minor issues. Write each one on its own slip of paper.

When you feel ready, burn each of the papers in the cauldron one at a time. Name the obstacle out loud as you light the paper and watch it burn. Notice if any signs or symbols reveal themselves to you in the burning of the paper. Repeat this process with each of the obstacles you have written down. You might even add one for the unseen obstacles that are in your way.

When all the papers are burnt to ash, add three pinches of salt to the ashes. Once the ashes are cool, stir this mixture in a counterclockwise direction with the first two fingers of your dominant hand. As you do, say:

Obstacles move from my path,
No need for worry or wrath.
The pathway is clear and ahead I move.
The way is open, the path is smooth.

When you feel ready, add some of the blessed water to the salt and ash mixture. Stir this with the first two fingers of your dominant hand in a clockwise direction. As you do, say:

Forward I move.
I'm in the groove.
It is easy and smooth.

Use this mixture to anoint the object of transformation. Speak your desires out loud as you anoint the object, seeing clearly that the road ahead is clear and open. Tell this talisman what its job and power is. Tell this talisman what you want it to do. Blow your breath across the talisman and activate the power of transformation within it.

Thank any guides and allies that you have invited into the ritual. Open up the energetic container that you created for the ritual. Pour the remaining water outside, just not on any plants. Carry the talisman with you. Once the ritual circle is open, take a moment to drink the Transformational Cassis Elixir and write down any important insights that came to you.

Blessed Water

You can use blessed water in the previous ritual or at any time. It is good to use to bless ritual objects or cleanse spaces. It is best to make this water on a full moon, but you can make it at any time in a pinch.

NEEDS

Ritual knife

1 teaspoon kosher salt

Large bowl of water

DIRECTIONS

Take your ritual knife and hold it in the salt, and say this:

I clear this salt of all negative energy.
May this salt bless all that it touches.

Pour the salt into the bowl of water and use your ritual knife to draw a pentacle in the water three times.

Transformational Cassis Elixir

This drink comes from Gwion Raven's book *The Magick of Food*. It is based on the story of Cerridwen and Gwion Bach. Both these beings go through massive transformation in the mythology. By drinking the elixir, we follow in their footsteps.

INGREDIENTS

For the lavender-honey simple syrup:

¼ cup boiling water

¼ cup dried lavender

⅓ cup honey

3 ice cubes

2 ounces brandy

1 ounce cassis (blackcurrant)

1 tablespoon lemon juice

Dash of bitters

Directions

To make the lavender-honey simple syrup, pour the boiling water into a bowl. Add the dried lavender and honey. Stir these three ingredients together and let steep for 30 minutes. After the 30 minutes are up, strain the syrup through a sieve or strainer to filter out the lavender bits. Extra lavender syrup can be stored in an airtight jar in the fridge for up to two weeks.

Add three ice cubes to a cocktail shaker. Pour in the lavender-honey syrup (one ounce), plus the brandy, cassis, lemon juice, and bitters, and give everything a good shake. Serve in a tumbled or stemless wine glass.

Creativity Ritual

Perform this ritual when you need to spark your creative self. If you have a new project starting up or want to increase your creative energy for any reason, this will help you get moving. After the ritual is complete, eat some Creativity Cake to finalize the ritual. Directions for the cake and the Creativity Oil follow the ritual.

Needs

Flowers

Cornmeal

3 taper candles in green, orange, and white (in candleholders)

A sharp stickpin

Cinnamon incense

Lighter or matches

Journal and pen

Creativity Oil (recipe follows)

Creativity Cake (recipe follows)

Directions

Create an altar space with all the items listed above and anything else you feel called to add to the space. Place the flowers in the middle of your altar space. Using the cornmeal, create a large triangle around the flowers. Have the candles and stickpin ready.

Light the incense to start and keep it burning throughout the entire ritual. Create an energetic bubble around your ritual space. Call in any guides and allies that you want to be a part of this ritual.

Pick up the stickpin and carve the word *creativity* into the green candle, the word *openness* into the orange candle, and the word *inspiration* into the white candle. Place each candle on one of the points of the cornmeal triangle.

Light the candles and allow the light of the flames to connect with your heart space. Imagine this triangle of magic connecting in with your heart and your heartbeat. Sink into the energy of creativity, and feel it moving in and around your body. Notice if there are any places of stuck energy or resistance, and allow the flames of the candles to burn through those places.

Continue to breathe and feel into the power of creativity within you. Allow yourself to find those stuck areas and use the power of the candles to move it, clear it, and get it out of the way.

Stay in this place for as long as you feel called. Let the candles burn down completely, and as they do, write down anything important or interesting that comes up. When you are done, anoint yourself with the Creativity Oil. Open the energetic barrier that you built around your space and have a slice of Creativity Cake.

Creativity Oil

Anoint yourself with this oil at the end of the ritual. It can also be used before starting any creative project. This formula is based on the Success Oil we make at my shop, Milk & Honey. You will need essential oils to add to a carrier oil, such as almond or grapeseed oil. This recipe makes ½ ounce of magical oil.

INGREDIENTS

5 drops lemongrass essential oil
2 drops rose essential oil
2 drops cinnamon essential oil
½ ounce base oil

Creativity Cake

Use this recipe to help you tap into your creative side or to ground after your creativity ritual. While you make the cake, feel the energy of creativity flowing through your hands and into the ingredients.

INGREDIENTS

1 egg
1 teaspoon orange flower extract
½ cup honey
2 tablespoons brandy
1 cup all-purpose flour
¼ teaspoon cinnamon
2 cups elderflowers
Fruit or whipped cream (optional)

Mix the egg, orange flower extract, honey, and brandy together in a bowl. Slowly stir in the flour and cinnamon. The mix should look like a thick pancake batter. Fold in the flowers.

Heat a griddle until hot. Pour a silver dollar amount of batter into the pan, and when bubbles start to rise, flip over the cake.

Top with fruit or whipped cream if desired.

Spirits Ritual

This ritual will help you connect with the Spirits of place, the entities that live where you live. You can do this ritual at any time, indoors or outside. There is a Spirit Oil to anoint yourself with before entering ritual space. You will find that recipe and a recipe for Spirit Crumble at the end of the ritual.

Needs

Spirit Oil (recipe follows)
Copal incense or your favorite incense
Lighter or matches
Small offering bowl
Milk, honey, and/or bread
Spirit Crumble (recipe follows)

Directions

Take a moment to breathe into your center and focus on the ritual. Create an energetic boundary around your ritual space. Anoint yourself with the Spirit Oil, then light the incense and hold the offering bowl in your hands.

If possible, sit in the middle of your living space or yard. Allow yourself to come to a place of stillness and slowly begin to expand your awareness. With each breath you take, allow the edges of your awareness to soften and expand, getting larger and larger in your living space.

When you feel ready, with your awareness expanded, see if you can connect with the spirit or energy of another entity in your space. This could be the spirit of your home, a fae being, a house spirit, an ancestor, or any number of beings. Take your time with this process. Allow it to slowly unfold and be patient. The energy you touch on might be subtle.

As your energy expands into your living space, you might not connect in with any energy. If this is the case, where might you imagine spirits of your place to be living?

Go with the offering bowl to the place where you feel the spirits or where you imagine they might reside. Pour the milk, honey, and/or bread and a piece of Spirit Crumble into the bowl. Speak out loud from your heart. Say what you want to the spirit of your place. Tell them that the offerings you are putting out are for them and express how you want to have a relationship with them. Notice if you get any signs or messages from the spirits of the place.

Stay in this place for as long as you feel called. Stay open to the process of communication. Notice whatever comes through.

When it feels complete, thank the spirits of the place. Put out the incense and open up your ritual space in whatever way you feel called. Leave the offering overnight. In the morning, pour the offering outside at a crossroads.

Spirit Oil

This recipe is based on the Wisdom Oil that we make at my shop, Milk & Honey. You will add drops of essential oils to a carrier oil, such as almond or grapeseed oil. This recipe makes ½ ounce of magical oil.

Ingredients

- 5 drops clary sage essential oil
- 2 drops sandalwood essential oil
- 1 drop rose geranium essential oil
- ½ ounce base oil

Spirit Crumble

This is an excellent dessert to help you replenish after an intense ritual. It's a great dish to take to a potluck or group gathering.

Ingredients

Water

5 cups mixed berries

2 tablespoons honey

2 tablespoons brown sugar

½ cup chopped hazelnuts

Ice cream or whipped cream (optional)

Preheat the oven to 350 degrees F. Fill the bottom of a small saucepan with about a quarter inch of water. Add in all the berries and cook over low heat for about 15 minutes. Wait until the fruits are soft but not overly mushy. Add the honey and brown sugar and mix until incorporated. Drain off any excess juice.

Spoon the berry mixture into a small baking dish and cover the fruit with the chopped nuts. Bake for 20 minutes or until golden brown. Serve warm and top with ice cream or whipped cream if desired.

Divination Ritual

When you need to open up your intuition and see clearly, perform this ritual. It is best done at night and does require a small space (like a closet) and no electric lights. I highly recommend using LED candles, as too many flame candles in a small space isn't good for your health and poses a fire risk. Use enough LEDs to light up the space so you are able to see.

Before starting the ritual, eat some of the Divination Pomegranate Sorbet to help you get into the right headspace. The recipe follows the directions for the ritual.

Needs

- 1 large black pillar candle
- Favorite incense or mugwort incense
- Lighter or matches
- Favorite divination system (tarot cards, oracle cards, runes, bones, etc.)
- Divination Oil (page 154) or myrrh essential oil
- Journal and pen
- Divination Pomegranate Sorbet (recipe follows)

Directions

Set up your space, making the room as dark as you can. Stand in the middle of the space and breathe deeply. Send out your energy to create a boundary around your ritual space. Light the black candle and incense. Keep the incense burning throughout the entire ritual.

Focus on the ritual at hand and then anoint your third eye with the Divination Oil.

Sit in silence for some time. As you sit, allow your awareness to open and expand. Breathe slowly and allow yourself to seek out a question that you desire an answer to right now. Where in your life do you need guidance or direction?

When the question is clear, take three deep breaths and ask your question out loud. Pick up your chosen divination system and perform a reading. Do this slowly and intentionally. Imagine you are performing this reading for another person.

Write down the answers that come through.

When you feel ready, thank your divination system and blow out the candle and incense. Slowly return to electric lighting or immediately go to bed and pay attention to your dreams to provide further insight.

Divination Pomegranate Sorbet

Pomegranates are a fruit connected to the underworld, and eating them can help you open up to the other realms more easily. This sorbet is perfect to eat before stepping into your divination ritual.

INGREDIENTS

2 cups pomegranate juice

⅓ cup orange juice

½ teaspoon lemon juice

1 tablespoon ginger juice

¼ cup white sugar

Pomegranate seeds, for garnish

Mix all the juices together in a container that can safely be frozen. Freeze the mixture for at least 3 hours. Once frozen, smash it up. With a mixer, beat the frozen mix until smooth. Put the mix back in the freezer for another 3 hours.

Once solid, scoop the sorbet into a glass and top with a sprinkle of pomegranate seeds. Serve immediately.

Courage Ritual

This is the ritual to perform when you need to boost your personal courage. It is best done on a full moon but can be performed any time you need it. Set up your ritual in a place where you can be undisturbed for at least an hour.

Directions for how to make Courage Oil appear after the ritual. This oil takes a month to make, so plan ahead. There is also a recipe for Courage Caraway Breadsticks to eat once the ritual is complete.

Needs

1 white candle, any size
Lighter or matches
Journal and pen
Handheld mirror
Courage Oil (recipe follows)
Courage Caraway Breadsticks (recipe follows)

Directions

Begin with a ritual cleansing in whatever way you prefer. Breathe into your center and focus on the present moment. Create a boundary with energy around your ritual space. Take a moment to call in any allies, guardians, or deities who can support you in this work. Remember to focus on courage and call in the spirit that helps you with that energy.

After you've called in your allies, light the candle and make some time to sit in a meditative state. Allow your awareness to focus on your authentic self. Are there any ways that you need to be more honest with yourself about your current situation? Are you asking for what you need? What feels out of balance, or what have you allowed to get out of balance?

Consider this question: What is my truth?

Write down what comes up around this meditation. Be honest and open with yourself. Take your time and allow anything that needs to be released to come out and flow onto the paper.

When you are ready, set down your journal and pick up the handheld mirror. Look at yourself. Really look at yourself and take your time. Pick up the Courage Oil and use it to anoint your throat. As you do this, say:

I say what I need from a place of authenticity.
I ask for what I need with courage and conviction.
I am what I am, I am what I am.
I deserve to be heard in my truth.

Write down anything else that comes up as you anoint yourself. Open your circle. Extinguish the candle. The work is done.

Courage Oil

This oil is used to increase courage, bravery, and internal power. After making the oil, you can use it to anoint yourself, magical objects, and spell objects. This recipe makes ¼ cup. You will need to add the herbs to a base oil such as grapeseed or almond oil.

Ingredients

Palmful of calendula petals

Pinch of dried peppermint

¼ cup base oil

1 small jar with a lid

Add the herbs to the oil in the jar and seal up the top. For the next thirty days, shake the jar every day. While you shake the jar, focus on courage and bravery. As you shake the jar, imbue that oil with the energy of bravery.

After thirty days, strain the herbs out and put the oil in a new jar.

Courage Caraway Breadsticks

Eat these breadsticks after your courage ritual.

Ingredients

1 package dry yeast

1 cup warm water, divided

1 tablespoon sugar

½ teaspoon nutmeg

2 teaspoons caraway seeds

1½ teaspoons salt

1 egg

¼ cup butter, softened

3 cups flour

Blend the yeast and ¼ cup of the warm water. Set this aside for ten minutes or until it starts to foam. Mix the rest of the warm water with the sugar, nutmeg, caraway seeds, and salt. Add the egg and butter to the mix, beating with a fork.

Sift in the flour and mix well. Cover the mix and put in the fridge for at least two hours, but better to let it sit overnight.

When the dough is done chilling, take it out of the fridge and divide it into three dozen small pieces. Roll these pieces into pencil-size strips. Place them on a greased baking sheet at least one inch apart and let rise for about 2 hours.

Preheat the oven to 400 degrees F. Bake the breadsticks for 10–12 minutes or until golden brown.

Making Changes Ritual

Sometimes we need to make changes, even if we don't know what those changes are. This ritual is best performed on a full moon. Several days before the full moon, start to contemplate the energy of this ritual. Focus on where you want to make changes or where it feels like change needs to happen. These changes could be due to a bad habit, a toxic relationship, a bad work environment, or anything else that you can feel needs to have a shift.

In the days leading up to the full moon, pay attention to your dreams. You may also want to perform a divination or spend time in meditation on the topic of change. Once you have clarity on the changes needed, write this down on a slip of paper.

After the ritual, have a cocktail to celebrate your changes. The mojito recipe for this ritual comes from the book *The Magick of Food* by Gwion Raven.

This ritual is best performed in or near a kitchen.

Needs

Hot water

Dried peppermint or a peppermint tea bag

Teacup

1 orange glass-encased candle

A Sharpie or glass marker

Your slip of paper

Matches or a lighter

Metamorphoses Mojito (optional—recipe follows)

Directions

On the night of the full moon, set up your ritual with all the items listed above at hand. When all the pieces of the ritual are ready, try to sit in a place where the light of the moon is shining down upon you. Make a cup of hot tea with some of the dried peppermint. As the tea is steeping, put a pinch of the peppermint on top of the orange candle.

Write your name on the glass of the candle, along with what it is you are ready to change. Add designs, symbols, or anything else that feels appropriate for the changes you want. Decorate the glass of the candle to help support what it is that you want to change.

Finally, put the slip of paper under the candle and light the candle. Allow the light of the candle to show you the possibilities of change and how these things will begin to manifest for you. Visualize that you are already living this life of change.

As the candle burns, write in your journal about these changes and how it feels to see a new life. Stay in this space for as long as you feel called, letting the candle burn the entire time. When it feels complete, snuff the candle and open your circle.

Over the coming days, burn the candle until it is finished.

Metamorphoses Mojito

This drink is based on the story of Menthe, who went through a transformation after being trampled under the feet of the goddess Persephone.

INGREDIENTS

- 1 dozen mint leaves
- 1 tablespoon lime juice
- 1 tablespoon honey
- Ice
- Sparkling water, tonic water, or lemon lime soda
- 1 slice of lime

Get yourself a tall glass. Add the mint leaves, lime juice, and honey and muddle them. To muddle ingredients means to crush them in order to release their oils and flavors. Add ice, your sparkling water of choice, and a slice of lime.

Past Lives with the Akashic Records

It's best to go into the hall of Akashic records with a plan. Otherwise it's much like going into a massive public library without an idea of what you want to read. You might find something that grabs your attention, but you are just as likely to wander around lost and then leave with nothing.

To take this journey, have someone read the following trance exercise to you or record yourself reading it and play it back for yourself.

Needs

A glass of water
Journal and pen

Trance

Cast a circle around your space in your favorite way. Relax and breathe deeply. With each breath, allow yourself to relax more and more. Allow tension to release and let your awareness begin to expand. As you breathe, notice that you are starting to sink into where you are sitting. You safely and comfortably sink deeper and deeper.

Your Witch's eye, that inner eye, begins to open as you sink down, and in front of you is a downward-spiraling staircase.

Begin to walk down the staircase. Place one foot in front of the other, step-by-step, moving down, down, down. Again you see the torches lighting as you approach, one foot in front of the other, step-by-step, moving down this spiral staircase.

You reach the bottom of the staircase and see in front of you a large, heavy door. On a small shelf next to the door is a pile of chalk. Pick up one of these pieces of chalk and write on the door "My Past Lives." Knock three times on the door and open it.

Inside the hall of Akashic records, directly in front of you, is a table. A large book appears. This book is the story of one of your past lives. This book might say your name from that lifetime on the front, or it might have a date, or possibly nothing will be written on the cover. Open the book and see what information is inside. This book might contain words, pictures, or images, or you might simply experience feelings when you look at the inside of the book.

Take time with what information is held in this book.

When you are finished looking at the book, close it. Turn and exit the hall of records. When you step through the doorway, the door closes behind you. Begin to climb back up the staircase, one step at a time.

Step-by-step you move up the stairs, one foot after the other. As you move up, up, up, the torches go dark as you move past them. With each step you become more and more aware of your physical body. That Witch's eye begins to close and you feel more and more connected to your physical body.

Breathe slowly and connect with your body. Slowly and gently open your eyes. Tap your edges and say your name out loud three times.

Conclusion

Spirit spells, recipes, and rituals are highly personal. The best way to improve your spiritual life is something that only you can know. Take the rituals and workings from this chapter and use them as inspiration to create your own. Growing spiritually is what life is all about. Let it be fun and adventurous for you.

Chapter 12

HOLIDAY RITUALS AND THE SPIRIT WHEEL OF THE YEAR

The Wheel of the Year resembles a wheel with eight spokes, with each holiday occurring at a different point in the year, spaced equidistantly apart. The center of this wheel is where we find Spirit. Remember back at the beginning of this book when we discussed that Spirit resides at the center? Well, here we see that concept materialize with the Witch's holidays and celebrations.

The Wheel of the Year has become a major part of the modern Witchcraft movement. One spoke happens about every eight weeks. Four points of the wheel happen at the equinoxes, around March 21 and September 21, and the solstices, around June 21 and December 21. The remaining four points of the wheel happen at the middle points between the equinoxes and solstices.

There is a lot of debate on when and how these markers on the calendar came about. A whole book could be written on the potential origins of these "holidays," but the history doesn't really matter to the modern celebrations.

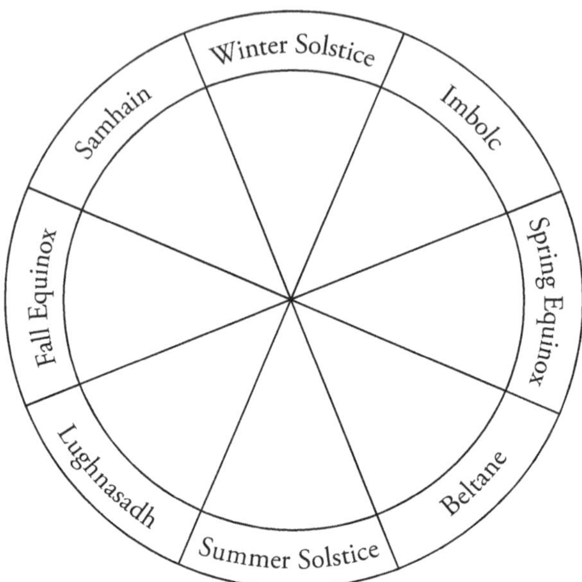

Just like all the topics we've covered in this book, we could argue that all the holidays on the Wheel of the Year are connected to the energy of Spirit. We move out from the center to connect in with the seasonal shifts and then bring our knowledge back to the center, continuing to move through the wheel over and over again.

The following celebrations feature a deity that can be worked with for that time of year, as well as craft projects, spells, cocktails, and recipes that you may want to incorporate into your seasonal celebrations.

Samhain

Some consider Samhain the end and the beginning of the year. Some even call this the Witch's New Year. In the Northern Hemisphere this day is celebrated on October 31, and in the Southern Hemisphere it is on May 1. In most modern Witchcraft traditions, this is a day to honor and celebrate our ancestors and our beloved dead. Samhain is the midway point between the Fall Equinox and the Winter Solstice.

Inanna

In the mythology of Inanna, who is a goddess from Sumer, she makes a journey to the underworld to meet her sister. Inanna is used to being Queen of Heaven and Earth and she possesses all the trappings of that title. When she reaches the gates of the underworld, she is told that she will need to release these trappings of power. There are seven gates she must cross to get to the underworld, and at each gate she is asked to remove another symbol of her power. The symbols are things like her crown, her lapis lazuli beads, and so on. Finally she reaches the underworld, stripped bare.

This story has a lot to teach us. What are the trappings that you hold to so dearly that don't actually matter in the long run? What are the titles, statuses, and beliefs that you hang on to about yourself that make you feel like you have power or importance in this world?

Samhain-tide, or the time of year around Samhain, is an excellent time to release old patterns, systems, and beliefs that no longer serve your highest good.

Inanna Ritual

Before performing this ritual, you will need to take some time to discover what your seven symbols of status are in your life. These objects could be things that you wear, like a wedding ring, or a representation of your business status, like a business card. These could also be things like a piece of clothing. If all else fails, write down the names or titles that you hold dear.

Needs

Athame or ritual knife

Dragon's blood incense or your favorite incense

4 glass-encased candles for the four quarters

Matches or a lighter

A candle of any size for Inanna

Music (optional)

Your seven objects of status

Journal and pen

Directions

You will need to set up a space to perform this ritual. Within the space, create a small altar with all the items listed above. Before beginning, take a few deep breaths and allow yourself to become fully present.

Light the incense. Pick up the athame and cast a circle around your ritual space in your preferred way. If you are unsure how to cast a circle, use your athame to draw a spiritual boundary around your ritual space.

When your circle-casting is complete, light each candle, and as you do, speak out loud to the element you are inviting in. Light the candle for Inanna and speak out loud to her from your heart. Ask for her guidance to help you release the trappings of who you are and step into your most authentic self.

If you are going to play music, now is the time to begin. One at a time, pick up each of the items you've collected. Hold this object in your hand and feel what it represents. How does this object (or title, word, etc.) make you feel? Where do you hold this energy in your body? Connect with this item and see where it shows up in your body. When you feel ready, set it down as if you are setting it down and releasing it from your life, knowing that once the ritual is done, you can easily pick it back up if you want to.

Take some time without the title or object. How do you feel now without this social trapping? How does it feel to be free of what this title means? Does this feel like a release or a loss? Notice how you feel different or the same. Take a few moments to write down what is coming up for you right now.

Repeat this process for each of the objects that you have gathered. Once you have released all these titles, take some time to feel into who you are now without them. Write down what feels important or interesting about this shift.

Sit in meditation or contemplation for as long as you feel called.

When you are ready, look at the objects you've set aside. Are there any of these titles or trappings that you want to leave behind? If so, don't pick those objects back up. However, if there are titles or objects that you are clear you want to keep with you, pick them up and honor how they add to your life. Take a moment of contemplation with each object that you are ready to continue to hold in your life.

When you feel complete, speak from your heart to Inanna, offering her your gratitude and thanks for witnessing your ritual. Extinguish her candle. Repeat this process with each of the elemental candles. Pick up the athame and open your circle in your favorite way.

If there are any objects that you want to leave behind after this ritual is over, you need to determine now how you will clear out this energy. Do you want to burn this object, donate it, offer it to another person, or recycle it into something new? Make plans to take care of these objects as soon as possible.

Apple Shrunken Heads

There's more to creeping out the neighbors on Halloween than just jack-o'-lanterns. Apple shrunken heads are very traditional and disturbing, perfect for Samhain decor. You will need at least six apples of any variety. Carve little faces into the apples. The little face doesn't need to go that deep into the fruit, just enough that you can tell it is there. As you carve your apples, put your oven on the lowest setting it will go. Place your apples on a cookie sheet lined with parchment paper. Place in the oven until the apples dry out. This could take a couple of hours.

Classic Pumpkin Pie

Pumpkins are a traditional food for Samhain-tide. This recipe is simple yet classic. Make it on Samhain and leave a slice out for your ancestors.

INGREDIENTS

1¾ cups pumpkin, cooked and mashed
½ teaspoon salt
1½ cups evaporated milk
⅔ cup packed brown sugar
2 tablespoons white sugar
1½ teaspoons cinnamon
½ teaspoon ground ginger
½ teaspoon ground nutmeg
¼ teaspoon ground cloves
2 eggs
9-inch piecrust

Preheat the oven to 425 degrees F. Beat the mashed pumpkin, salt, evaporated milk, brown sugar, white sugar, and all the spices together until the mix is smooth. Beat the eggs separately and then add to the pumpkin mix. Pour the mix into the piecrust. Bake the pie for 15 minutes and then turn the heat down to 350 degrees F. Bake for another 30–40 minutes or until the top is golden and the mix is solid.

Underworld Drink

This cocktail is inspired by the energy of the underworld and dancing with the beloved dead. Mix these up on Samhain night to celebrate the ancestors.

INGREDIENTS

2 ounces bourbon

½ ounce lime juice

½ ounce simple syrup

Dash of bitters

Ice

Ginger beer (to top)

Combine the bourbon, lime juice, simple syrup, and bitters. Mix well and pour over a glass of ice. Top with ginger beer.

Winter Solstice

Around December 21 in the Northern Hemisphere and June 21 in the Southern Hemisphere, we reach the point of the least amount of daylight. This is a time to celebrate the dark and sing back the sun. This is the darkest point of the year, and starting the next day, we begin to gain back a bit of daylight each day.

The Winter Solstice is a good time for dreaming in the dark. It is an excellent time to hibernate and slow down. At the darkest time of the year, see how you can best reserve your resources, for the rest of the winter is still ahead.

Skadi

Skadi is the Norse goddess of winter. What I mean by that is she is the actual winter, not just a representation of it. Skadi is actually one of the ice giants and was fine living her life on her own. In the myths, due to the killing of her father, Skadi is offered marriage to the god of the sea, Njord. As you can imagine, the goddess of winter and mountains and the god of the vast ocean are not necessarily compatible. The two end up spending most of their time apart.

Rather than live her life unhappy, Skadi admits that she needs to be in the cold mountains. She wants to be where her heart calls to her, not stuck at the wet sea. The Winter Solstice is also a good time to go within and make sure you are honoring what it is your heart truly wants.

Skadi Ritual

Although the Winter Solstice might not be the deepest time of the winter season, it is the darkest point of the year. To honor the shifting of the seasons, perform this ritual for Skadi.

Needs

Athame or ritual knife

Winter incense, like pine or evergreen

Lighter or matches

A glass-encased candle for Skadi

A drum or rattle

Bowl of snow or ice

Journal and pen

Directions

Breathe with intention, allowing yourself to shake off any distractions and be present with the ritual at hand. Use your ritual knife to create an energetic boundary between your ritual and the outside world. Light the incense. Light the Skadi candle. As you light the candle, speak out loud to the goddess, inviting her into your ritual space. Ask her to share her guidance on getting through the coldest and darkest parts of the year.

Sit in contemplation with the drum or rattle. Play a steady rhythm and allow the power of Skadi to fill your ritual space. Let your eyes go soft and open up your Witch's eye, that eye that sits above and between your normal seeing eyes.

When your Witch's eye is open, you can better hear, see, and sense the messages that Skadi might have for you. Continue to drum and take your time with this process. If you have specific questions about getting through the darkness, ask them now. See what answers Skadi can offer you. Be in this place of contemplation as long as you need to.

When you feel ready, anoint yourself with the snow or ice from your altar. Take a moment to honor Skadi and any wisdom that she may have offered to you. Thank her for joining your ritual and then extinguish her candle.

Open your circle in your favorite way, then write down anything important or interesting that may have come up in your ritual.

Winter Solstice Candleholders

If you don't want to go to the fuss of making a Chocolate Yule Log Cake (recipe follows) at the Winter Solstice, you can make these candleholders and use them every year! Making these candleholders will require power tools, so if you aren't used to using power tools, you may need to get some assistance.

INGREDIENTS

A large natural log, whatever type of wood you prefer, about the size of a small baby

3 long taper candles

Hole saw to fit the candles

Spray varnish

Holly leaves, berries, or other winter decor and a glue gun (optional)

Directions

Figure out how you want the log to lay. However you place the log, make sure it is steady and won't rock or tip. Drill three holes for the candles, equidistant apart. Make sure that whatever size of candles you use will fit in the holes that you create. The best type of candles are long tapers. Spray the log with varnish to keep it from decomposing.

If you want to decorate the log with holly leaves, berries, or other winter decor, you can use a glue gun to attach these items. Put the candles in the holes and place the log on your Winter Solstice altar.

Chocolate Yule Log Cake

The Chocolate Yule Log Cake is not an easy thing to make. If you want to make one for an event, you may want to practice a time or two beforehand to make sure you've got the hang of it. Although it's tricky, it is a beautiful showstopper and delicious too.

Cake Ingredients

¾ cup all-purpose flour

⅓ cup dark cocoa powder

1 teaspoon baking powder

½ teaspoon salt

4 eggs, whites and yolks divided

¾ cup sugar

2 tablespoons cream cheese

3 tablespoons sour cream
¼ cup melted butter
1 teaspoon vanilla extract

WHIPPED CREAM FILLING INGREDIENTS

1¼ cups heavy whipping cream
¾ cup powdered sugar
1 teaspoon vanilla extract
⅛ teaspoon salt
8 ounces soft mascarpone cheese

WHIPPED CHOCOLATE GANACHE INGREDIENTS

8 ounces semisweet baking chocolate, chopped fine
1 cup heavy whipping cream

Preheat the oven to 350 degrees F. Line an 18-by-12-inch jelly roll pan with parchment paper. Whisk the flour, cocoa, baking powder, and salt in a large bowl. Whisk the egg yolks and sugar in a separate large bowl until fully combined. Add the cream cheese, sour cream, melted butter, and vanilla extract to the yolks and sugar mixture. Mix until fully combined and set aside. In yet another bowl, beat the egg whites until they form stiff peaks. Gently fold ⅓ of the egg whites into the cocoa mix. Once combined, fold in the rest of the egg whites. Spread the batter into the pan and bake for about 10 minutes, testing every few minutes.

When the cake is fully baked, lift it out of the pan and carefully roll it with the parchment paper while it is still hot. Set it aside until fully cooled.

Once the cake is totally cool, you can start to make the filling. With a mixer, combine the heavy whipping cream, powdered sugar, vanilla extract, and salt until stiff peaks form. Then fold in the mascarpone cheese.

Very slowly unroll the cake. Spread the filling evenly on the cake and then carefully roll the cake back up without the parchment paper. Carefully wrap the cake in plastic wrap and set in the fridge with the seam down.

While the cake sets, make the chocolate ganache. Place the chopped chocolate in a bowl and set aside. Heat the heavy whipping cream in a small pot on the stove until just boiling. Pour the hot cream over the chocolate and let sit for a few minutes. Stir the mixture until fully combined. Let the mix cool and then whip it with an electric mixer.

Take the cake out of the fridge and cut three inches off one end. Set that piece on the side of the log so it looks like a smaller branch. Slather the chocolate ganache over the cake until it is fully covered. Use a fork to create bark-like markings on the ganache. You may want to add leaves or berries to the cake for decoration. Keep the cake in the fridge until you are ready to serve it.

Peppermint Stick Martini

Make this cocktail to keep you warm on a long, cold Winter Solstice night. It is an excellent drink to have at the end of the Skadi ritual to warm you up.

Ingredients

2 ounces vanilla vodka

1 ounce chocolate liqueur

1 ounce peppermint schnapps

Ice (for the shaker)

Crushed candy canes for the rim of the glass (optional)

Shake all the ingredients together on ice. Top the glass rim with crushed candies. Drain the drink into the glass.

Imbolc

For many traditions, this is the time of year when we start to acknowledge that springtime is coming. In the Northern Hemisphere this event falls on February 1, and in the Southern Hemisphere it takes place on August 1. Imbolc is the midway point between the Winter Solstice and the Spring Equinox. In many traditions, this holiday is connected to the Irish goddess Brigid.

Brigid

Brigid is a Celtic goddess whose stories show up across most of the Celtic world. There are many stories and myths connected to this goddess, and she was often thought of as a literal part of the land. There are groves of trees, hillsides, wells, rivers, and waterways all given the name of Brigid, in one form or another.

Many modern Witchcraft practitioners connect the goddess Brigid with the celebration of Imbolc on the 1st or 2nd of February, which also happens to be the celebration of Saint Brigid in Ireland. One of the sacred energies that Brigid holds is that of midwife, and this time of year is when the lambs are foaling. We often see images of Brigid with lambs because of this connection.

In the Reclaiming Tradition of Witchcraft, we often make pledges to the goddess Brigid at this time of year. It's just enough past New Year's that it feels like a really good and thoughtful New Year's resolution but without all the pressure.

Brigid Ritual

Before performing this ritual, determine what you wish to pledge for the coming year. Is there a goal you'd like to set? Is there a habit you'd like to break or strengthen? Is there a specific change you want to dedicate yourself to at this time? Once you have clarity on your pledge, start the ritual.

Needs

- Athame
- Cedar incense or your favorite incense
- Matches or a lighter
- 4 glass-encased candles for the four corners
- A candle of any size for Brigid
- A heat-resistant container (like a cauldron), with a lid
- Enough Epsom salt to fill an inch of the bottom of the cauldron
- Enough rubbing alcohol to cover the salt plus a half inch
- Bell or chime
- Journal and pen

Directions

Start the process by setting up your ritual space. Make sure you are in a place where it is safe to have a fire. Outdoors is best. Place your cauldron in the middle of the ritual space, along with all the other items listed above.

Breathe deeply and feel into the land around you. Pull in any energetic threads that feel disconnected or distracted. Pick up the athame and use it to create an energetic barrier between your ritual and the outside world. Light the incense and then light each of the candles for the four corners, speaking out loud to each of the elements, inviting them to join your circle.

Light the candle for Brigid and speak out loud to her, inviting her into your ritual space. Make sure to mention that you are calling her to witness your pledge and you are making this pledge as an offering to her.

Pour the Epsom salt into the bottom of the cauldron about two inches thick. Pour the rubbing alcohol over the salt until there is about a fingernail length above the salt. Light the alcohol on fire. It should burn for at least thirty minutes.

While the fire burns, contemplate your pledge. You may want to dance around the fire. You may want to sing. Do whatever you feel called to do at this time. Use this time as a moment to pay homage to Brigid and the pledge you are making.

When you feel ready, approach the cauldron and focus on your pledge. Make sure your words are clear and concise. Breathe into your pledge and feel its energy. When you feel ready, speak the pledge out loud. Ring the chime and feel it reverberate through you.

Sit with your pledge and the cauldron fire in front of you. Expand into this feeling and sit in this place for as long as you feel called. If you need to extinguish your cauldron fire, simply place a lid on top of the cauldron. Extinguish the candle for Brigid, and as you do, speak out loud to Brigid. Offer your gratitude for her being a part of your ritual.

Extinguish all the elemental candles, offering your thanks to each of the elements. Use your athame to open your circle in your preferred method. Write down anything important or interesting that may have come up in your ritual.

Ice Candles

I remember making ice candles when I was in elementary school. We made them as a Christmas gift for our parents. I gave mine to my dad, and he had it out on a shelf all the time for years. It's super easy to make these candles and fun to do with kids.

Needs

- Double boiler with a bowl that will only ever be used for melting wax
- Water

Chunks of wax

Coloration for candles (wax melt colors or remnants of colored crayons)

Bottom quarter of a half-gallon cardboard milk carton

A candlewick

A pencil

Ice cubes

Sprigs of greenery or other decor (optional)

Directions

Heat the water in the double boiler and put the wax pieces in the bowl. As you wait for the wax to melt, cut up the milk carton. Make sure it is clean and dry. Tie one end of the candlewick to a pencil and place it in the middle of the milk carton.

When the wax is melted, add in the coloring you desire. Fill the milk carton bottom with ice and then quickly pour in the hot wax. When the ice melts, pour off the excess water. If you hear any water trapped in the wax, poke a small hole in the wax and pour it out.

When the candle is fully set, peel off the milk carton, and there you have an ice candle! You can use sprigs of greenery or other decor to add some design to the candle.

Brigid Cheese Board

This is a really simple recipe. All you need are three to six different cheeses and three to four different meats. If you are unfamiliar with cheese, go to your local upscale grocery store that has a cheese counter. Ask the person working there to help you pick out some cheese. You want at least one soft cheese, one hard cheese, and a sheep cheese. You may also want to add some cured olives, sliced apples, and two different types of nuts.

When you have all your ingredients together, get out a wooden chopping board. Place all the items you've collected on the board in a way that is pleasing to look at. Put out some small cheese knives for the different cheeses and some toothpicks to help pick up items.

Eat it all yourself or bring it to a ritual.

Snowdrop

Winter may still be here, but we can toast to the coming of spring. As someone who lives where it doesn't snow, I love this drink to connect me with the colder climate that I don't get to experience.

INGREDIENTS

2 ounces vodka

1 ounce lime juice

½ ounce blue curacao

Ice

Soda water

Mix all but the soda water with ice. Strain into a chilled glass and fill the glass with soda water.

Spring Equinox

The Spring Equinox happens around March 21 in the Northern Hemisphere and September 21 in the Southern Hemisphere. This is a day of balance. We have the same amount of daylight as darkness and it is just before the moment when we swing into the warmer part of the year. Hotter days are ahead and the peak of the year is still ahead of us too.

Eostre

There is mythology connected to a deity called Eostre, which was the Anglo-Saxon word for the modern month of April. The German folklorist Jacob Grimm connected an obscure goddess named Ostara to the word Eostre. Although some modern folklorists have disputed this claim, there are still many modern Witchcraft and Pagan practitioners who connect the Spring Equinox with Eostre and Ostara.

The legend speaks of a spring goddess who was so beautiful that as she walked upon the earth, the land would wake up and start to blossom. Her energy was that of springtime. All the creatures of the forest were deeply in love with this goddess because of her beauty. One woodland creature wanted to prove his love to the goddess. A young rabbit went through the forest collecting different-colored eggs as a gift to the springtime goddess.

Eostre Ritual

Perform this ritual when you are ready to connect with the energy of spring. What is important about this ritual is to keep it regional; use what you have access to where you live. Before starting the ritual, consider whom you might want to offer a springtime blessing.

Needs

- An assortment of flowers in season
- Your favorite incense
- A candle for Eostre
- Matches or a lighter
- Brown paper or newspaper

Directions

Set up your ritual space where there is a large table or space to create with the flowers you've collected. Ground and center yourself. Take a moment to feel into the energy of the spring. You might even want to look outside and see what spring looks like at this exact moment.

Light the incense and the candle for Eostre. As you light the candle, speak from your heart to Eostre. Ask for her assistance in honoring the energy of the springtime.

Create squares with the paper and begin to put together small arrangements of flowers. Make as many small arrangements as you have people on your list for offering spring blessings. When all your arrangements are completed, use the incense to bless these bundles. Ask Eostre to bless the flowers.

Clean up your ritual space and then head out to deliver your spring blessings. It's best if you can leave them where they will be found. Consider leaving these blessings on car windows, front doors, or anywhere they will offer a surprise to the person receiving the blessing.

Natural Egg Dyes

When our kids were young, we would celebrate the Spring Equinox together by decorating eggs and having a picnic, and we would use natural materials to dye the eggs. The longer you keep your eggs in the dye, the more dynamic the color will be. Make sure you hard-boil the eggs first.

Ingredients

Hard-boiled eggs

Water

2 cups shredded beets (for red to pink colors)

2 cups red onion skins (for red to orange colors)

2 cups yellow onion skins (for orange colors)

¼ cup turmeric (for yellow colors)

2 cups chopped purple cabbage (for blue and purple colors)

2 cups blueberries (for blue colors)

White vinegar

Boil two cups of water with each color ingredient. After about half an hour of boiling, strain the water and add a tablespoon of white vinegar for each cup of colored water. Soak the eggs for at least two hours in the colors you desire. If you want to mix and match, you'll need more time to allow the colors to be brighter. Dry off the eggs and there you go! Beautiful enough for Eostre herself.

Springtime Quiche

Eggs are so much a part of the springtime. They are a reminder of how sacred life is. Eggs are truly connected to Spirit. In many traditions, the cosmic egg is where the entire universe came from.

INGREDIENTS

9-inch piecrust

1½ cups grated cheddar cheese

¼ cup sliced mushrooms

¼ cup chopped tomato

¼ cup chopped ham

4 eggs

1 cup half-and-half

Preheat the oven to 350 degrees F. Cover the bottom of the piecrust with the cheddar cheese. Mix the vegetables and meat together and pour over the top of the cheese. Thoroughly beat the eggs and the half-and-half together and pour this mixture into the piecrust. Put in the oven and bake for 1 hour or until cooked through and golden brown on top.

Spring Gin Garden

This drink is refreshing and fun. It could be the perfect addition to a springtime picnic or celebration.

INGREDIENTS

1 ounce dry gin

½ ounce strawberry liqueur

½ ounce lemon juice

Sparkling wine (topper)

Pour the ingredients through a strainer into a chilled glass and then top with sparkling wine.

Beltane

The height of spring happens in the spot between the Spring Equinox and the Summer Solstice. This point on the Wheel of the Year is called Beltane. It takes place on May 1 in the Northern Hemisphere and November 1 in the Southern Hemisphere. This day is a celebration of fertility, growing life, and all the promise of spring.

There is a tradition of getting up early on May Day morning to cover your face in the fresh dew. The belief is that if you do this, your skin will appear youthful and healthy. You just have to set your alarm to wake you before dawn.

Bacchus

Bacchus is the Roman counterpart of the Greek god Dionysus. They have a lot in common, but there are also some distinct differences. Both are gods of the vine, ecstasy, and indulgence. However, Dionysus is often depicted as youthful and androgynous. The indulgence he offers is to heighten spiritual revelation and disconnect from the status quo. Bacchus is depicted as an older, bearded man, often heavy-set. He represents all the things that excess can bring. Both gods remind us of revelry, celebration, and reconnecting with nature.

Bacchus Ritual

This ritual is designed for a group of people to tap into the energy of revelry. Wine or alcohol can be included in this ritual if appropriate for your group of people. However, this ritual can easily be performed without alcohol. Determine ahead of time who would be a good energetic addition to this ritual. When you send out the invites, ask everyone to bring food and drink to share with the group.

Set up your ritual space with intention. Consider the setup of the space, the lighting, the comfort of the room, and even the temperature. You want the ritual space to feel lush and comfortable. Have lots of options for seating.

Create a playlist of music. You might want to curate a playlist that is fun, wild, and upbeat or more sensual and slow. In my opinion, the best type of playlist is one that follows a flow of energy. It starts out slow and builds and then comes back down.

Needs

- Food and drink
- Athame or thyrsus (a pinecone-topped wand)
- Lemongrass incense or your favorite incense
- Candles to add ambiance lighting to the space
- A glass-encased candle for Bacchus
- A way to play your music list

DIRECTIONS

When everyone has arrived and you have the food and drink set out, invite all participants to join you in setting up sacred space.

Start with a grounding. If you have a favorite method, use it. Otherwise, say this:

> *Take a deep breath and connect with the Earth below you. Feel your roots sink into the Earth and allow them to go as deep as you feel called. Maybe your roots go all the way into the center of the Earth, or maybe they stay close to the soil at the top of the planet. Let your roots go where they need to be and take a moment to breathe with the Earth below you.*
>
> *On your next breath, release anything that doesn't need to be here. Send anything you are ready to release into the Earth, where it can be composted. When you feel ready, call up the Earth's energy. On each breath, pull up the Earth energy into your body. Let that energy fill you up as it moves upward. Feel that energy move up your legs and fill your pelvic bowl. Pull that energy into your ribs, and arms, and neck, and face. Allow that Earth energy to flow all the way into the top of your head, where it rains out the top of your head and down around you, clearing out your auric field.*
>
> *When you feel ready, allow your roots to come back into your body. Slowly open your eyes and let yourself be here now.*

After the grounding, cast a circle around your ritual space. If you have a favorite way to do this, do that casting. Otherwise, do this:

Pick up the athame and go to the east. Hold the athame up and say: *By the Air that is his wild song.*

Use the athame to create an energy barrier, moving from east to south. Hold the athame up in the south and say: *By the Fire that is his intense passion.*

Continue to move in a circle around your ritual space from the south to the west. Hold up your athame in the west and say: *By the Water that is his deep emotions.*

Move from the west to the north, continuing to create an energetic barrier. When you reach the north, hold up your athame and say: *By the Earth that is the vine.*

Return to the east to complete the circle. Move to the middle of the ritual space, point your athame above you, and say: *By all that is above.*

Point your athame at the ground and say: *By all that is below.*

Set your athame on the altar and say: *The circle is cast. We are between the worlds and what happens between the worlds changes all the worlds. Let the revelry begin!*

Light the incense and the candles for lighting. Light the candle for Bacchus and say:

We call in the wild God. We call in the revelry. We call in the vine. We call in the magic that is so divine. We call upon Bacchus. We call upon the vine. We invite in the party and the song and that is so divine.

Turn on the music and allow things to unfold. Pour the drinks, eat the food, and dance to the playlist.

This ritual could take hours to complete. Just allow it to unfold as it does, without trying to shape it or push it. When it feels complete and people are clearly reaching the end of their energy, it's time to close up the ritual and open the circle.

Start by thanking all the participants of the ritual. Turn off the music. Extinguish any candles you have lit for lighting and the incense if it is still burning. Finally, blow out the candle for Bacchus and say:

Thank you for your song. Thank you for your joy. Thank you for bringing your power, your life force, and the ritual to enjoy. Hail and farewell, Bacchus.

Pick up the athame and acknowledge the below and the above. Then move to the east and begin to pull back the curtain of the circle you've created. Turn counterclockwise, using the athame to cut open or pull back the circle.

Hail and farewell to the ritual.

Maypole

Maypoles are a traditional way to honor this time of year in many Anglo-Saxon areas of the world. Traditionally the maypole was a ritual for fertility, but there are many Christian communities that create maypoles without the connection to fertility. This is not a solo activity. You will need at least six people, but more is better.

To create a maypole, head to the hardware store and get a thick wood pole that is about seven feet tall. If you have a lot of people who will be dancing around the maypole, you might want to make it taller, like ten feet or so. You will also need many different-colored ribbons, one for each participant of the may dance. The easiest thing to do is use an eye screw at the top for ribbon attachment. You can screw this hardware into the top of the pole and tie one end of each ribbon to the screw.

You will need to create a hole at least two feet down into the ground. A post hole digger will make this process really easy. Put the pole in the hole and use the soil you pulled out to fill in around the pole and make it secure.

Spread the ribbons out, giving each participant a ribbon. Have all the participants stand at the end of their ribbon, holding it securely but not too tight so it doesn't pull on the pole.

Then comes the tricky part. It's best to have an even number of people for this dance. Have everyone pair off, with each pair facing each other. Everyone going clockwise will go "under" the ribbon and everyone going counterclockwise will go "over" the ribbon. This becomes a pattern of "over" and "under" as each person approaches another person. The people are creating the weave of the ribbons around the maypole.

The more people who are dancing the pole, the more likely this will get a little chaotic. In my experience, it starts out calm, gets chaotic and messy, then rights itself and the weave of the ribbons ends up being beautiful and magickal. It helps to have music, a song, or a chant for people to sing or listen to. This helps to keep the dance feel exciting and raise some energy.

Ham and Calendula Sandwiches

There's nothing better on Beltane than a picnic with high tea and finger sandwiches. This is a simple recipe, easy to make and quick to disappear.

Ingredients

8 ounces cream cheese

2 tablespoons mayonnaise

1 tablespoon horseradish
3 teaspoons lemon juice
2 tablespoons relish
1 apple, diced
1 cup calendula petals
1 piece of flatbread
1 cup thinly sliced ham
Calendula flowers, for garnish

Mix the cream cheese, mayo, horseradish, lemon juice, and relish in a bowl. Once totally mixed, gently add in the diced apple and calendula petals. Gently spread the mix over the bread and top with the slices of ham. Chill until serving. Garnish with calendula flowers.

Merry May Drink

This is a light and refreshing drink, perfect to have after dancing the maypole. It can be made in a big batch as long as you shake before serving.

INGREDIENTS

2 ounces white wine
½ ounce fig liqueur
Dash of bitters
Ice
Edible flowers, for garnish

Shake the ingredients with ice. Strain into a glass and garnish with an edible flower.

Summer Solstice

The height of summer happens on the Summer Solstice. It is the point of the year when we experience the most daylight. In the

Northern Hemisphere this happens around June 21, and in the Southern Hemisphere it takes place around December 21. This is the height of the summer's energy. For those of us in the United States, school is over for the summer and we are honoring Father's Day right around this time.

Ra

Ra was the sun god of ancient Egypt. That is to say, Ra was *the* sun for the people of ancient Egypt. He was the being that carried the sun from horizon to horizon every single day. In the desert, the sun is a powerful part of life, one that brings life and can also easily take it away. As you might imagine, there are many stories, myths, and legends of Ra.

Ra Ritual

On the Summer Solstice, we have the greatest amount of daylight for the entire year. It is an excellent time to celebrate the sunshine and the power of the summer. The energy of the sun is all about power, selfhood, and courage. Use this day to honor and connect with these powers that already exist within you. This ritual is best done in the middle of the day with a small group of people.

Needs

- Comfortable clothes
- Towels or blankets
- Sunscreen
- A sun umbrella
- Journal and pen
- Offering for Ra

Directions

Head outside on the Summer Solstice. Find a place where you want to sit and enjoy the day. This could be in your backyard or a public park or anywhere you are excited to visit on the solstice. Lay out your blankets, put up the sun umbrella, and set up your space to be as comfortable as you desire.

Create your sacred space in your favorite way. This could be as simple as acknowledging the four elements and Spirit. Call Ra into your circle and/or acknowledge the sun above you. Offer gratitude to the sun for providing warmth, light, and energy to our world. Express to the sun how much you appreciate its power. Apply sunscreen as a celebration of the solstice. Lay out in the sun and feel the power of the sun. Notice the power of the sun around you and how much we need the sun and how much it does for our lives.

Journal anything that comes up. Leave an offering for Ra and express your gratitude. When it feels complete and you're ready to go back indoors, close up your ritual space in your favorite way and thank Ra for his power.

After Sun Skin Cream

Use this cream after you've spent a day out in the sun. It not only can help with a sunburn but can also hydrate and smooth skin if irritated. You will need a double boiler or a glass bowl set on top of a pot of boiling water.

Ingredients

1 cup coconut oil

1 tablespoon beeswax

1 tablespoon cocoa butter

1 tablespoon olive oil

1 cup aloe vera

Heat the water in a double boiler and put all the ingredients except the aloe vera in the bowl. Stir often while the ingredients melt together. Once all the ingredients are melted, take the bowl off the heat and set aside. Once the mixture has cooled but is still slightly warm, add the aloe vera and mix again. You may need to use an electric mixer for this process. Store in an airtight container and use as needed. If properly stored, this cream can last up to six months.

Summer Cool as a Cucumber Soup

This cold soup is a delish addition to any Summer Solstice party, ritual, or gathering. It is also cooling and refreshing, great for a hot day.

INGREDIENTS

2 tablespoons butter

3 large cucumbers, peeled and sliced

1 onion, chopped

2 tablespoons lemon juice

2 cans cream of celery soup

1½ cups water

⅓ cup sour cream

Chopped dill, for garnish

Melt the butter in a skillet and add the cucumbers and onion. Cook slowly until the cucumbers are tender, but do not brown them. Using a food processor, blend the mixture with the lemon juice until you get a froth. Add the cans of soup, water, and sour cream and blend again until smooth. Chill the soup until ready to serve.

Summer Slide

This is a fun summer drink with a hint of coffee. It will help you stay up until the wee hours of the night, well after the Summer Solstice sun has gone to bed.

INGREDIENTS

1 ounce light rum
½ ounce cherry liqueur
½ ounce coffee liqueur
Dash of bitters
Ice

Shake and strain the ingredients over ice.

Lughnasadh

Lughnasadh is also referred to as Lammas, which translates to "loaf mass" in modern English. Lughnasadh is the ancient Celtic term for the harvest time of the year, while Lammas is a Christianized version of the celebration, often jokingly called the bread holiday. There are connections between this time of year and the harvest, which is where the bread comes in. But this was also a time when the ancient Celtic peoples gathered for trade and games of skill. Some connect this time of year with the Irish god Lugh, who was known in myth and legend to be "many skilled." This day is most often celebrated on August 1 in the Northern Hemisphere and February 1 in the Southern Hemisphere.

Lugh

In Irish mythology, Lugh is the god of craftsmanship. He is a brave, strong warrior, and his weapons are the spear and the sling-stone. In the stories, Lugh is celebrated as the inventor of games and horse racing. He is a major figure in Irish mythology and is one of the greatest heroes of these tales. He is the original jack-of-all-trades, known for being highly skilled in anything he attempts to do.

Lugh is the sun god, bringing joy and happiness with him. He is known to offer oracles and speak prophecies in the form of poetry. As Lugh is the god of the sun, it is no surprise that he is also the god of the harvest. The date of Lughnasadh coincides with the middle of the harvest season.

As Lugh is a deity of poetry, many skills, and oaths, it is no wonder that his holiday sits exactly opposite Imbolc, a holiday with strong connections to the goddess Brigid. Brigid possesses many of the same skills that Lugh is known for.

Lugh Ritual

One of my favorite ways to celebrate Lughnasadh is with a day of games. A good old-fashioned field day is one way to honor the day of skill, but as someone who doesn't like field day, I like to do a hybrid of field games and board games. This ritual should be done outdoors during the day, with some covered space. This is a ritual for a medium-size group.

Needs

- Field games and board games
- Food and drink
- A small altar for Lugh, with prizes for the games and an image of him

Directions

Set up the field games out in the open and the board games in a covered area. Set up an area for food and drink and encourage attendees to bring some to share. Set up your altar for Lugh, making sure the altar is well out of the way of any gameplay.

When all are gathered, create sacred space in your favorite way. Call upon Lugh to witness the games and lend his many skills. Have someone in the group offer a blessing for the food and drink that has been shared.

Play games, eat and drink, and have a great time. When it feels like the event is winding down, thank Lugh for joining your rite. Open your ritual space in your favorite way and clean up the ritual space.

Food Altar

One of my favorite rituals is the food altar ritual. When I was involved with a public ritual planning group, we would often have a food altar for our Lammas gatherings. This altar can be created for you, a small group, or a large public gathering. The key is to get the word out to attendees to bring food to share and any harvests from personal gardens.

Before the ritual begins, create a tablescape with a large table; boxes, stands, and crates to create different heights; and lots of fabric. Cover the table, boxes, stands, and crates with different fabrics and then begin to add the decor. This could be flowers, fresh vegetables, jars of local honey, and plates or platters of food. As each person arrives, they add to the altar. Then during the ritual, everyone can eat from the altar.

Harvest Corn Bread

Corn might be ready to harvest at this time of year, but depending on where you are, it might still be a few weeks away. This recipe is best with fresh corn.

Ingredients

- 2 cups all-purpose flour
- 2 cups cornmeal

1 tablespoon baking powder

1 teaspoon salt

3 tablespoons sugar

4 eggs

2 cups buttermilk

½ cup corn oil

1 cup freshly cobbed corn kernals

Preheat the oven to 350 degrees F. In a small bowl, mix together the flour, cornmeal, baking powder, salt, and sugar. In a separate bowl beat the eggs. Whisk the buttermilk, oil, and kernels into the eggs. Pour the egg mixture into the dry ingredients and mix until totally combined. Don't overmix.

Pour the mix into an 8-by-11-inch baking dish that has been greased. Bake for one hour or until a toothpick inserted into the middle comes out clean. Cool on a wire rack.

Harvest Punch

This punch is perfect for when you are ready to celebrate the harvest but you need just one drink to help you get through the rest of the hard work.

Ingredients

2 ounces single malt whisky

½ ounce sweet vermouth

½ ounce elderberry syrup

Ice

Stir all the ingredients together and pour over ice.

Autumn Equinox

The Autumn (or Fall) Equinox sits at the opposite side of the year as the Spring Equinox. In the Northern Hemisphere this day falls around September 21, and in the Southern Hemisphere it happens around March 21. Again, just like the Spring Equinox, this is a day of balance. We have an even amount of daylight and darkness on the Autumn Equinox. However, unlike the Spring Equinox, after this day we move into the darker time of the year and the winter is close at hand.

Persephone

Persephone starts off as a spring maiden but ends up falling in love with the ruler of the underworld, Hades. Through this relationship, she becomes Queen of the Underworld. Her myth was a major part of one of the biggest spiritual traditions of the ancient world, the Eleusinian Mysteries. These mysteries explored her descent into the underworld and her ascent when she returns to the world above.

Persephone Ritual

Persephone holds a lot of power connected to both the spring and the dead. The purpose of this ritual is to meet with this goddess and gain any insight that she holds for you at this time. Before this ritual, consider what you might want to ask her about. Persephone holds the energy of the growing things and the dying things.

For the journey part of the ritual, you may want to record this part ahead of time and play it back during the ritual. Otherwise, you can have someone read the journey for you.

NEEDS

Ritual knife or athame

Candles of any size for the four elements

Matches or a lighter

Incense such as lotus, rose, or anything floral

A candle of any size or color for Persephone

Journal and pen

Directions

Take deep breaths and focus on the work at hand. Then use your ritual knife to create an energetic barrier between you and the outside world.

Light the candles for the elements, and as you do, speak out loud a welcome to each of these energies. Light the incense. Light the candle for Persephone and speak from the heart to invite her energy into your ritual space.

Let yourself get comfortable and then listen to the following meditation.

The Journey

Breathe slowly and with intention. Allow each breath to be a message to your body to relax and open up to Spirit. Allow each breath to come slowly and deeply. Allow each breath to open and soften your edges.

As you relax and release, allowing your edges to soften and widen, begin to open your Witch's eye, that inner eye that sits above and between your normal seeing eyes.

As that Witch's eye opens, you see before you a path. You begin to follow this path, putting one foot in front of the other. Take one step and then another, following the path deeper and deeper into the place of mystery.

As you walk, you see a beautiful spring meadow and a cave ahead of you. As you approach, the scent of blossoms fills the air and the buzzing of bees reaches your ears. As you get closer to the cave's entrance, a cool breeze brushes against you. Take a few moments to explore this meadow and the cave's opening. (*Pause here.*)

You hear a noise and feel a shift and a shake, and you see that from the opening of the cave a form begins to appear. This is Persephone, spring maiden and goddess of the underworld. She begins to move forward, and as she does, she becomes more solid, clear, and sharp. Persephone moves forward to greet you. Take some time to speak with this goddess and see what information she has for you. (*Pause here.*)

When you feel ready, ask the question that you are holding in your heart and see what Persephone has to tell you. This answer might come in the form of words or images. You may experience the message in a feeling, or a scent, or a whisper. Allow the answer to come in whatever form it may. (*Pause here.*)

Remember that our time in this realm is limited. Although you cannot stay here much longer, you can return at any time to speak with Persephone. If you haven't already, take some time to express your gratitude to her for the information she has offered to you tonight. (*Pause here.*)

Persephone moves back toward the cave, and as she does, she begins to disappear. You turn and walk back to the path that brought you here. Allow your feet to carry you forward, one foot in front of the other, step-by-step. As you follow this path, your Witch's eye begins to return to its normal state of being.

As that Witch's eye begins to close, you start to feel the edges of your body come back into a firm place. You notice your edges and your body and your breath. When you feel ready, slowly open your eyes and look around your ritual space. If you need to, use the palms of your hands to tap the edges of your body and come fully back into the present moment.

If you have been lying down, slowly sit up. Take a moment to write down anything important or interesting that may have come up during your journey.

When you feel ready, begin to close down your sacred space. Blow out the candle for Persephone and speak from your heart to release her energy from your circle.

Follow this same pattern with each of the elements. Blow out each candle and speak your gratitude from your heart to each of the elements for being present in your ritual.

Finally, take the athame and open the circle in your favorite way.

Welcome back!

Straw Pentacle Wreath

For this project, you can use a store-bought wreath or you can use branches and long grains to create your own round wreath. This project is best done with a group of coven members or Craft friends.

Needs

- Wreath
- Harvest decorations
- A glue stick with a glue gun

Directions

You can go to a craft shop and pick up the decorations that you find appealing or go for a walk in nature and wildcraft some decor for your wreath.

Lay out all the items that you've collected in one space. Heat up the glue gun and start to have fun with it. Use the hot glue to affix items to your wreath.

Acorn Cookies

These cookies are a traditional rollout sugar cookie. You will need an acorn-shaped cookie cutter and frosting or icing in whatever form you desire, but these cookies are great without any type of topping! They do need to sit in the fridge overnight, so make sure you plan ahead.

Ingredients

2 cups sugar

1 ½ cups soft butter

4 eggs

1 teaspoon vanilla extract

5 cups flour

2 teaspoons baking powder

1 teaspoon salt

Frosting or icing (optional)

Start by beating the sugar and butter together, creating a creamy texture. This is best done with an electric mixer. Add the eggs and vanilla extract and continue to beat the mixture until combined. Gently stir in the rest of the ingredients until fully combined. Cover with plastic wrap and put in the fridge. For best results, leave overnight.

The next morning, preheat the oven to 400 degrees F. Dust your rolling surface with flour, and dust your rolling pin too. Roll out the dough to about a half-inch thickness. Use the acorn cookie cutter to cut out your cookies, and place them about an inch apart from each other on a cookie sheet covered with parchment paper.

It should take about 5 to 8 minutes for the cookies to bake to a light golden brown color. When they have the right color, move them over to a cooling rack and wait until they are totally cool before adding any frosting or icing, which, of course, is totally optional.

Tipsy Pumpkin Spice Coffee

Stay warm on the inside and out, all while sipping some delicious pumpkin spice.

Ingredients

1 cup hot coffee

3 tablespoons pumpkin puree

¼ cup warm milk

¼ teaspoon pumpkin pie spice

2 ounces dark rum

Whipped cream (optional topper)

Combine all the ingredients except the rum and whipped cream, and stir thoroughly until combined. Stir in the rum. Top with whipped cream if desired.

Conclusion

The Witch holidays are meant to be fun and celebratory. Including food, drink, and merriment is all part of a good holiday. Let these rituals and recipes be a jumping-off point for your own spirit to connect with the Wheel of the Year and create magick for your world and life.

CONCLUSION

Although not all Witchcraft traditions work with Spirit as an elemental force, they all work with the energy of Spirit. Spirit is a part of everything we do. Spirit is what weaves the other four elements together. Spirit is the animating force that holds the universe together. Whether you call this force Quintessence, dark matter, the unknown, or Spirit, we all feel its imprint on our magical world.

In Astrea Taylor's book *Air Magic*, she mentions that none of the elements exist in a vacuum. However, Spirit does. Spirit is the vacuum. But I do agree with her that the best magical practitioners will understand that a balance between all the elements is needed, and Spirit is a part of that balance too.

Air helps us know, think, and process. It also helps us with our words and communication. Fire can help us with our relationship to willpower. Fire is passion, movement, and energy. Water helps us be daring. It is emotional, intuitive, and deep. Earth reminds us when it is best to keep silent. It is grounding, stable, and solid.

Spirit is all these things and none of these things. Spirit is the thing that moves between the other elements, connecting them with magic.

I hope this book helps you remember the magic that is all around you. When you incorporate Spirit into your magical practice, you step into the flow of what many of our magical predecessors called Quintessence. Spirit is the magic that science has not yet been able to explain. When you cast a circle, you honor the element of Spirit. Spirit animates your spells, connects you to the gods, and helps you remember that you are a spiritual being having a human experience.

Our magical practices really aren't complete without Spirit.

May the force (Spirit) be with you.

ACKNOWLEDGMENTS

It takes a lot of people to transform a book from an idea into a tangible, physical thing. This is my eighth book and I'm still amazed at the amount of teamwork needed to complete this type of project. I literally could not have done it on my own.

First of all, thanks to Heather Greene for being a badass editor and ally. I'm so grateful that you considered me for this project. Having my writing accepted by Llewellyn is a humbling blessing. You are a kind and supportive force, and I'm grateful to know you. Thanks to the editors, designers, media folks, and skilled professionals at Llewellyn who have helped make this book a reality. There are many magical fingerprints throughout these pages.

Thanks to Dodie Graham McKay, Astrea Taylor, Lilith Dorsey, and Josephine Winter, who all contributed pieces to this book. It literally takes all the elements to make Spirit move.

Thanks to my kiddo who has supported me through the writing of every book. I appreciate your pick-me-ups. I appreciate your gifts. And I love Alfredo Fredichini. He was my ride or die through the creation of this book.

Thanks to my kitten boy Spike for hanging out with me in the office, distracting me with your cuteness, meowing for attention, and generally making me adore you.

Finally, thanks for the reality TV show playing in the background while I edited and cleaned up this manuscript. If not for the trash television that is *Love Island*, I don't know that I would have finished writing this.

Appendix

SPIRIT CORRESPONDENCES

Keywords	Liminal, Aether, Quintessence
Direction	Center
Seasons	The between seasons
Times of Day	Dusk and dawn
Astrological Signs	All of them and none of them
Planet	Jupiter
Tarot	The major arcana
Chakras	Hands and feet
Tool	Cauldron
Incense	Myrrh or frankincense
Elementals	None

Colors	Black, white, silver
Gems	Angelite, larimar, seraphinite (See more in chapter 7.)
Plants	Althea, eyebright, marigold, thyme (See more in chapter 6.)
Tree	Yggdrasil, or the world tree
Animals	Mythological animals (See more in chapters 2 and 8.)
Deities	Charon, Heimdall, Janus, Neith (See more in chapter 3.)
Sense	Sixth sense
Symbol	Pentagram
Rune	Odin's rune, or the blank rune
Magical Lesson	To take magick into the world

BIBLIOGRAPHY

Alpenglow Expeditions. "A Brief History of Mt. Shasta." Accessed August 2025. https://alpenglowexpeditions.com/blog/a-brief-history-of-mt-shasta.

Andrews, Ted. *Animal Speak*. Llewellyn, 1996.

Auryn, Mat. "The Veil Between the Worlds." *For Puck's Sake.* Last updated December 17, 2018. https://www.patheos.com/blogs/matauryn/2017/10/11/the-veil-between-the-worlds.

Beckett, John. "Thinking About the Veil Between the Worlds." *Under the Ancient Oaks.* Last updated October 25, 2020. https://www.patheos.com/blogs/johnbeckett/2020/10/thinking-about-the-veil-between-the-worlds.html.

Brenner, Kelly. "Folklore & Nature: Dragonflies." Migratory Legends. September 25, 2019. https://www.metrofieldguide.com/folklore-nature-dragonflies.

Britannica. "Multiple Souls." Accessed August 2025. https://www.britannica.com/topic/multiple-souls.

Cabinet. "The Fifth Element and Medieval Cosmology." Accessed August 2025. https://www.cabinet.ox.ac.uk/fifth-element-and-medieval-cosmology-1.

Chapman, Fred. "Medicine Wheel/Medicine Mountain: Celebrated and Controversial Landmark." WyoHistory.org. April 10, 2019. https://www.wyohistory.org/encyclopedia/medicine-wheel.

Conway D. J. *Magickal Mystical Creatures*. Llewellyn, 2003.

Crawbuck, Allison, and Rhys Everett. *Spirits of the Otherworld.* Prestel, 2021.

Cunningham, Scott. *The Complete Book of Incense, Oils & Brews.* Llewellyn, 1986.

Cunningham, Scott. *Cunningham's Encyclopedia of Magical Herbs.* 1985. Reprint, Llewellyn, 2020.

DeLay, Michael Shilo. "The Life and Death of the Aether (Part I)." DemystifySci, June 23, 2025. https://demystifysci.com/blog/lifeanddeathoftheaether.

Dorsey, Lilith. *Water Magic.* Llewellyn, 2020.

Edgar Cayce's A.R.E. "Edgar Cayce on the Akashic Records." Accessed August 2025. https://edgarcayce.org/edgar-cayce/readings/akashic-records.

Encyclopædia Britannica editors. "Abu Simbel." Britannica. Accessed August 2025. https://www.britannica.com/place/Abu-Simbel.

Encyclopædia Britannica editors. "Western Wall." Britannica. Last updated August 1, 2025. https://www.britannica.com/topic/Western-Wall.

English Heritage. "History of Stonehenge." Accessed August 2025. https://www.english-heritage.org.uk/visit/places/stonehenge/history-and-stories/history.

Exploratorium. "Frog Myths." Accessed August 2025 https://annex.exploratorium.edu/frogs/folklore/folklore_4.html.

Farrar, Janet, and Gavin Bone. *Lifting the Veil.* Acorn Guild Press, 2016.

Farrar, Janet, and Stewart Farrar. *A Witches' Bible.* Phoenix, 1996.

GoldenTempleAmritar.org. "The Golden Temple Amritsar." Accessed August 2025. https://www.goldentempleamritsar.org.

Great Tibet Tour. "Kunlun Mountains." Accessed August 2025. https://www.greattibettour.com/tibet-attractions/kunlun-mountains.

Hall, Judy. *The Crystal Bible*. Walking Stick Press, 2003.

Hawkins, Jaq D. *Elemental Spirits*. Crossed Crow Books, 2024.

History.com editors. "Halloween 2025." History. Last updated May 28, 2025. https://www.history.com/topics/halloween/history-of-halloween.

Johns Hopkins Medicine. "The Brain-Gut Connection." Accessed August 2025. https://www.hopkinsmedicine.org/health/wellness-and-prevention/the-brain-gut-connection.

Jordan, Michael. *Encyclopedia of Gods: Over 2,500 Deities of the World*. Echo Point Books & Media, 2022.

Kerns, Tom. "Plato's Three Parts of the Soul." Philosophy 101. Accessed August 2025. https://philosophycourse.info/platosite/3schart.html.

Kershner, Kate. "What Are Ley Lines?" HowStuffWorks. Updated November 30, 2023. https://science.howstuffworks.com/science-vs-myth/unexplained-phenomena/ley-lines.htm.

Keys, Helen. "Hares in Celtic Mythology." Mallon Ireland. February 28, 2022. https://mallonireland.com/blogs/news/hares-in-celtic-mythology.

Kynes, Sandra. *Llewellyn's Complete Book of Correspondences*. Llewellyn, 2013.

LeFae, Phoenix. *Hoodoo Shrines and Altars*. MISC, 2015.

LeFae, Phoenix. *What Is Remembered Lives*. Llewellyn, 2019.

Lipp, Deborah. *The Elements of Ritual*. 2003. Reprint, Llewellyn, 2021.

Mankey, Jason. "The Witches' Pyramid." *Raise the Horns.* Last updated December 26, 2018. https://www.patheos.com/blogs/panmankey/2018/12/the-witches-pyramid.

Mark, Joshua J. "The Soul in Ancient Egypt." World History Encyclopedia. March 2, 2017. https://www.worldhistory.org/article/1023/the-soul-in-ancient-egypt.

McKay, Dodie Graham. *Earth Magic.* Llewellyn, 2021.

Michelle, Heron. *Elemental Witchcraft.* Llewellyn, 2022.

Muse Spells. "Turtles in Mythology." August 18, 2022. https://medium.com/@musespells/tortoises-turtles-in-mytholog-ba0209f654e2.

Musei Vaticani. Sistine Chapel. Accessed August 2025. https://www.museivaticani.va/content/museivaticani/en/collezioni/musei/cappella-sistina/storia-cappella-sistina.html.

Naydler, Jeremy. *Temple of the Cosmos.* Inner Traditions, 1996.

New World Encyclopedia. "Axis Mundi." Accessed August 2025. https://www.newworldencyclopedia.org/entry/Axis_Mundi.

Nicholas, Chani. *You Were Born for This.* Harper One, 2020.

Oregon Explorer. "Facts About Crater Lake." Accessed August 2025. https://oe.oregonexplorer.info/craterlake/facts.html.

Oxford Reference. "Triloka." https://www.oxfordreference.com/display/10.1093/oi/authority.20110803105721221.

Pamita, Madame. *Baba Yaga's Book of Witchcraft.* Llewellyn, 2022.

Pepper, Elizabeth, and John Wilcock. *Magical & Mystical Sites.* Harper & Row, 1977.

Polson, Willow. *Sabbat Entertaining.* Citadel Press, 2002.

Prabhu, Nilesh. *The Compendium of Mythical Creatures.* Self-published, 2023.

Pruitt, Sarah. "9 Powerful Snakes from History and Mythology." History. Last updated May 28, 2025. https://www.history.com/news/snake-symbol-history-mythology.

Raven, Gwion. *The Magick of Food.* Llewellyn, 2020.

Riess, Adam. "Dark Energy." Britannica. Accessed August 2025. https://www.britannica.com/science/dark-energy#ref1025335.

Spiller, Jan, and Karen McCoy. *Spiritual Astrology*. 1998. Reprint, Atria, 2010.

Taylor, Astrea. *Air Magic.* Llewellyn, 2021.

Therapeutic Shamanism. "The Shamanic Journey: A Journey to the Three Shamanic Realms." March 18, 2022. https://www.therapeutic-shamanism.co.uk/blog/shamanic-realms.

Uluru Australia. "What Is Uluru?" Accessed August 2025. https://uluru-australia.com/about-uluru/what-is-uluru.

Valiente, Doreen. *The Charge of the Goddess.*

Varanasi. "History." Accessed August 2025. https://varanasi.nic.in/history.

Vulture Conservation Foundation. "The Symbolic Representation of Vultures Across Civiliations—A Review." May 12, 2017. https://4vultures.org/blog/the-symbolic-representation-of-vultures-across-civilizations-a-review.

Wen, Benebell. "Hermetic Lots (Arabic Parts)." BenebellWen.com. Accessed August 2025. https://benebellwen.com/astrology-2/hermetic-lots.

Wigington, Patti. "Spider Mythology and Folklore." Learn Religions. December 23, 2018. https://www.learnreligions.com/spider-mythology-and-folklore-2562730.

Winter, Josephine. *Fire Magic.* Llewellyn, 2021.

Wilkes, Isobel. "Hares in Roman Art by Isobel Wilkes." Corinium Museum. Accessed August 2025. https://coriniummuseum.org/2021/08/hares-in-roman-art-by-isobel-wilkes.

Wood, Jamie, and Tara Seefeldt. *The Wicca Cookbook*. Celestial Arts, 2000.

Zakroff, Laura Tempest. *The Witch's Cauldron*. Llewellyn, 2017.

INDEX